WOMEN WITHOUT HUSBANDS

Women without Husbands

An Exploration of the Margins of Marriage

Joan Chandler

St. Martin's Press   New York

First published in the United States of America in 1991

Printed in Hong Kong

ISBN 0–312–06107–2

Library of Congress Cataloging-in-Publication Data
Chandler, Joan.
Women without husbands: an exploration of the margins of marriage
/Joan Chandler.
p. cm.
Includes bibliographical references and index.
ISBN 0–312–06107–2
1. Single women. 2. Marriage. 3. Family. I. Title.
HQ800. 2.C45 1991
306.81—dc20 90–26212
CIP

Contents

Acknowledgements

The ideas that form the heart of the book emerged from a research project on women married to naval servicemen. Here I would like to thank Colin May and David Dunkerley for facilitating the research, Devon County Council for funding it and the many women who participated in it. In the development of the book I am particularly grateful to Janet Finch and Jo Campling. Throughout the entire project I am especially grateful to Lyn Bryant for her unfailing support and encouragement.

JOAN CHANDLER

1

Women without husbands: an introduction

There have been many discussions of the relationship between men and women inside conventional marriage. But what is their interrelationship outside conventional marriage and how does women's marginality to marriage influence other aspects of their lives? These are the central questions of this book. Single women are categorised by type of non-marriage, as in the widowed, the divorced, and the never-married. Nevertheless there are definitional problems in establishing who women without husbands are. Many never-married women cohabit and may act as married or quasi-married and be treated as such. On the other side of the official marital divide there are married women who live alone. Changing marriage patterns and the longevity of women are increasing the numbers of women without husbands and blurring the boundaries of marriage and non-marriage.

Aside from the categories of women without husbands there are also issues of the ways in which marriage influences the lives of women who are not conventionally married. At its broadest, marriage touches all adults, heterosexual and homosexual alike, and shapes the socialisation of children. Marriage is seen as central to family life, permeating the law, tax structures and labour markets, shaping the identities of men and women and providing the social backdrop for the care of children. In Western society, marriage means 'coupledom' and this is widely influential on the non-married. The preference for sexual and domestic pairing is widespread. Homosexuals who do not live alone typically live as couples, and some have pressed the church with greater or lesser success to bless their unions as marriages. The couple is central to household organisation and heterosexual couples who live together are commonly treated as married.

1

The influences of marriage may touch all but are more keenly felt by women. This reflects their relationship with children, the links between femininity and wifehood and their residual role as economic dependants. Women are socially licensed by marriage to bear and rear children. Lesbian and single women may become mothers and with the increased availability of reproductive technologies this may be accomplished without entering into relationships with men. But the social emphasis remains on appropriate motherhood, and the control of inappropriate pregnancy is effected through policing women's sexuality and fertility and linking both to marriage. The residual identity of marital dependant ensures that women are more married than men inside marriage and affords them less autonomy when they are outside marriage. Discrimination against women in the public domain is often rationalised by their close connection with marriage and domesticity. For all women marriage casts a long shadow, part of the way in which they are defined and categorised by their relationship to men. Wifehood is keyed into womanhood to socially stigmatise those who are unmarried. In this way the structure and ideology of marriage are central to the gendering of women.

The issues become even more sharply defined where women were previously married or are cohabiting. They have a heritage of marriage or, in law and custom, a quasi-married relationship with men. They are also women whose household routines and life-course decisions have been, or continue to be, organised about the residential presence of a man. In the idealisation of the nuclear family there is a clear delineation: women are either married or they are not. In reality women not only have a variety of marital statuses, they also have a range of domestic and sexual relationships with men. In short, there are degrees of marriage. There is a broad and varied group of women outside conventional marriage but with some domestic connection to men. The group includes those who are no longer married, the separated, divorced and even the widowed, as well as women who cohabit with men without being married to them. It also includes women whose marriages are partial or intermittent, where husbands are away for occupational or custodial reasons, leaving women to function as *de facto* lone wives, and single parents, women who are mothers without being wives. The influence of marriage on the lives of women is not an issue of *category* but of *degree*. Its symbolic and material influences stretch to shape the lives of those furthest from marriage, as with never-marrying never-cohabiting women, but these influences are more keenly felt by women with the closest sexual and domestic connection to men.

What is at issue in this debate is not a particular woman's position on the continua of marriage, but the nature on the marital continua along which women are placed and the common ground of being more or less marginal to marriage, more or less connected to men. While the literature contains increasingly coherent accounts of women's experiences in marriage, those beyond it have been targeted as special groups with particular problems where discussion has emphasised their unique circumstance, such as divorce, bereavement, unmarried motherhood or cohabitation. It has fragmented discussion and individualised problems.

By contrast, this book attempts to describe the recurring issues in women's experiences outside conventional marriage, since much of the diversity is variation on similar themes and these themes derive from the nature of marriage. Marriage then becomes a question of degree where women in a wide variety of domestic circumstances are given a place within a broader and more coherent approach to family life. The issues are clearer for widows, divorcees, cohabitants and women whose husbands are regularly absent from home. The book concentrates its discussions on these particular examples of women without husbands while recognising that its conclusions may be more or less extended to all women outside conventional marriage.

The discussion is also an analysis of family life in change. The nuclear family provides an ideology of household organisation, kinship relation and sexuality which underpins a domestic structure composed of a breadwinning husband, a homemaking wife and their dependent children. Increasingly these types of domestic arrangements appear transitory or looser in their formulation. Although eight out of ten women presently marry, many will become divorced and even more become widows. In recent years there has been a steady increase in the numbers of children born to single mothers and a growing preference for cohabitation. Even among the married population, many women will experience spells of husband absence. This amorphous group of women exiting from marriage or living in incomplete marriages deserve more recognition, both because of their numeric weight and because most women in the course of their lives will experience some, if not all, of these marital and quasi-marital states and relationships.

The book has a number of purposes. First, it aims to demonstrate that conventional marriage may be a transitory or non-existent relationship as, for the truly uninitiated in the study of family forms, this is an essential starting-point. It intends to explore the experiences of women with more tenuous relationships to men who live in a society still structured around the assumptions of the nuclear family. This exploration has been made possible with maturing feminism. Over the past two decades feminist thinking has created a major place for itself within sociology and one of its key concerns has been women's familial experience and its continuity with other areas of social existence. Feminist thinking problematises our understanding of family forms and its relationship to women. Gittins (1985) questions the essential nature of 'the family', nuclear or otherwise, and emphasises the cultural and historical variability of domestic relationships between men, women and children. The feminist critique also goes beyond a neutral accounting of diversity, challenging the idealisation of nuclear family forms, deconstructing family units and peeling back the myths of family life to uncover the reality of women's experiences inside conventional families (Barrett and McIntosh, 1982). The task is now to examine the lives of women who are peripheral to conventional families.

Second, the discussion is a critique of assumptions that theories of the family can be broadened in some egalitarian way to include atypical families. The nuclear family has become synonymous with 'the family', and as such is not a neutral concept, but one that idealises conventional family forms and problematises women outside marriage and those in less conventional relationships. Thus 'the family' clouds our perception of women's experience inside marriage and distorts our vision of the lives of women outside marriage. As an ideological filter for domestic experiences, 'the family' generates false comparisons in the relative assessment of different women's lives. Women without husbands live in the shadow of 'the family' and this shadow has a double impact, structuring their experiences and altering our perception and analysis of those experiences.

Third, 'the family' supports an ideology that has clear material repercussions, influential on women inside and outside marriage. It structures domesticity, childcare and sexuality and it shapes economic dependence and relations with the state. The bulk of the literature catalogues the problems of women without husbands, but marginality to marriage may also bring a real growth in personal autonomy for women.

Fourth, 'the family' adds contradiction to women's lives and feminism has done much to uncover the ambivalence and ambiguity it generates: women are homemakers who work; their marriages are partnerships in which they are economically dependent; women lean on men and yet are the main carers, the pillars of everyday life; marriage assumes love and romance, but it is also a legal and an economic contract. The tensions between family responsibility, marital dependence and personal happiness are endemic in conventional families. The question that emerges is whether the circumstances of women who do not live in conventional families are similarly shaped, or whether women's experiences on the fringes of marriage are discontinuous with those of ordinary married women.

Fifth, it must be remembered that the model of the conventional family is also one that is white and bourgeois, but as family form is mediated by class and ethnicity so women's experience outside marriage is similarly influenced. Marginality to marriage has different implications for the poor and the black as opposed to the better-off and the white and the variability in the lives of these women may not stem only from differences in their domestic relations with men.

Finally the study of women without husbands is not only important in its own right but also provides an analytic vantage point from which to view normal marriage. An analysis of this group offers a fresh critique of marriage, not from inside conventional conjugality, but a view from the periphery, an alternative vista on wifedom and womanhood. In theoretical terms distance can heighten visibility. This links to the argument of Smart, who chose to examine patriarchy and the law on marriage through the analysis of divorce, since 'the reality of women's relationship with men inside the family is revealed at the stage of divorce or breakdown' (1984, p. 12). In disintegration the tensions of marriage bubble to the surface and the ties between husbands and wives are clarified in their disengagement or reformulation. Some of the penalties and privileges of marriage disappear, but more are re-shaped.

There is commonality as women without husbands are seen as social anomalies and often as social problems, becoming a focus of public concern and state interest. They are major recipients of welfare benefits, objects of social suspicion and butts of sexual innuendo. Also the single-parent family is a synonym for moral breakdown and social disorder. It is not just that their personal troubles have become public issues, but that the way in which they are seen and dealt with by public agencies rebounds to re-frame their personal experience. The privacy of the family is a privilege of the conventionally married and the behaviour and relationships of women marginal to marriage are more closely scrutinised and carefully policed by social workers and welfare agencies and their problems are more likely to be dealt with by counsellors and doctors. Hence practitioners concerned with family matters are frequently absorbed in the lives of those marginal to marriage.

As the lives of women outside marriage shadow those of women inside, a range of issues emerge, each more or less influential on the circumstances and experiences of women without husbands and each meriting attention. Marginality to marriage influences their personal lives, their household routines, their economic circumstances and their access to, and use of, wider social support. Conventional families composed of husband, wife and children have a three-cornered structure. As daily ties between husband and wife loosen or disintegrate children typically remain with women and lone wives become lone mothers. All these issues are crucial. Finally, the dynamics of marriage for any individual woman may not only be towards its loosening, but also towards its tightening. Women may remarry or husbands return. Within this process new families may be formed and blended and the bonds of conventional family life strengthened or retied.

An examination of the family forms that develop around quasi-marriage and non-marriage is overdue. Although partial and dissolved marriages do not exist in a social and economic vacuum, as they are not constituted independently of marriage itself, their understanding is a major developmental task for the sociology of families and 'the family'. As the book offers an account of marriage from its periphery, the discussion will begin with an analysis of the changing pattern of marriage before turning to an examination of the rich variety of women who live on its margins.

Changing patterns of marriage

Marriage is a normal and expected part of female biography in Western society. However, although the vast majority of women will expect to marry at some time and at least once, in recent years there has been some decline in the popularity of marriage. In 1971 only 4 per cent of women remained unmarried by 50, but by 1987 the proportion had grown to 17 per cent (Kiernan and Wicks, 1990). Women today are marrying older and marrying less and the trend may foreshadow other changes in household organisation and family formation.

Historically, the rate and timing of marriages has fluctuated and in pre-industrial Britain the average woman delayed marriage until her late twenties and about a fifth would not have married at all. Marriage then, as now, was tied to the structure of the economy and the ease of securing a living within it, with couples encouraged to delay marriage until they could sustain and support an independent household. In the twentieth century when industrial prosperity and wage labour gave younger people viable incomes, the chances of marrying increased and the average age for marriage fell to its lowest point in the 1960s. Always sensitive to economic factors, over the past decade the trend has reversed, couples are marrying later, teenage marriage has sharply declined and the average age for spinsters to marry has crept back up to twenty-four (Haskey, 1987). The rise in age of marriage influences the measurement of marriage overall, depressing global rates and giving an impression of decline. There are also suggestions from the USA (Bennett, Bloom and Craig, 1989) and Scandinavia (Popenhoe, 1987; Hoem and Hoem, 1988) that contemporary marriage rates there are on the decline.

In the twentieth century, divorce rates have steadily increased in the western world, peaking in the war and when divorce legislation changed. Today a third of marriages presently being formed will end in divorce within fifteen years. Along with the highest marriage rate, Britain now also has the highest divorce rate in the European Community, with each year thirteen divorces for every thousand existing marriages. Since 1961 the divorce rate has increased more than sixfold, while in the same time-period France's rate rose threefold to reach eight per thousand and Germany's increased almost two and a half times to approach nine per thousand (*Social Trends*, 1989). Nevertheless Britain's divorce rate is surpassed by that of the USA where twenty-two out of every thousand marriages dissolve annually.

However, direct extrapolation from marriage and divorce rates to instability in domestic relationships is rarely valid. These rates measure the changing structure of marital status and may be a poor guide to the coherence of domestic relationships. It could be claimed that changes in divorce law may have increased the symmetry between unofficially dissolved and legally dissolved marriages, with increases in divorce leading to a fall in unofficial separation. Chester (1972) attempted to test this hypothesis in an analysis of women's applications for maintenance and welfare as set against the divorce rate, and found that both had risen. He concluded that levels of informal separations had increased as well as divorce. However, this type of approach does not circumvent the problems of constructing reality through official statistics as, for instance, it rests upon an assumption about women's consistent propensity to claim support from partners and the state.

The growth of divorce may not connote the trivialisation of marriage but its increased significance, with more intolerance of imperfections and the unremitting search for the right partner. Being a divorcee may be seen as a brief interlude in people's lives: three-fifths of divorced husbands and half of divorced wives whose marriages ended between 1975 and 1982 were remarried within three years (*Social Trends*, 1989). The popularity of marriage also overrides its dissolution and the picture we have of levels of marriage is complicated by the incidence of remarriage. In recent decades the marriage market has been kept buoyant by the increased proportions of second and subsequent marriages. In 1961, 14 per cent of all marriages in the United Kingdom were those in which one or both partners had been married before. In 1988 the proportion had increased to 36 per cent (*Social Trends*, 1990), figures comparable to those found by Schofield and Wrigley (1981) for sixteenth-century Britain.

Nevertheless, remarriage rates fall dramatically for women over forty and are presently declining among all the divorced. And, although remarriage may signify the continued importance of marriage, the failure of more than half of these marriages adds grist to the argument for marital instability and an inflationary factor to divorce figures, as in 1986 nearly a quarter of divorces in Britain involved at least one partner who had been married before.

Changes in the global rates for remarriage also reflect the population structures of those eligible. The marriage rate for men who have lost partners has fallen by a third since the early 1970s to fifty-eight per thousand, whereas in the same period the remarriage rate for women has declined slightly from twenty-five to twenty-two per thousand. The lower rate for women reflects the large numbers of elderly widows and female divorcees whose chances of remarriage are small.

The divorced population is concentrated in younger age groups and in 1986 the highest proportion of divorced women, one in ten of the age group, were found among women aged 35–44. Among elderly women widowhood predominates – of those aged 65–74 in 1986 over a third were widows and less than 4 per cent divorcees, and among those over 75 nearly two-thirds were widows and less than 2 per cent divorcees. Furthermore widows accounted for over half the women in their late fifties who live alone, a figure which rises progressively with age. Because of their relationship to age, widowhood and divorce are problematised in different ways. Nevertheless, as the current cohort of divorced women in their middle years become older, such distinctions will be harder to draw and the 'problem' of divorce will be extended.

Cohabitation also appears to have grown; Haskey and Coleman's work found that 12 per cent of the population cohabit at any one time and a third of all couples have cohabited at some time (1986). The growth of cohabitation in part compensates for the decline of marriage. Kiernan and Wicks (1990) 'estimate that, for the 1980s, around half of the reduction in the proportions of women ever-married at ages 20–24 and one third of the decline at ages 25–29 could be accounted for by the increased propensity to cohabit' (p. 9). Cohabitation in Britain has an important transitional status as demographic analysis also identifies cohabitation as a popular prelude to marriage and aftermath to divorce. While 7 per cent of the women aged 18–49 were cohabiting in 1988, the numbers rose to 12 per cent among those aged 18–24 and to 27 per cent among divorced women (*General Household Survey*, 1989). Also the time spent cohabiting is lengthening among the once-married and this is the age group for whom cohabitation is becoming a long term alternative to marriage.

There has also been an increase in the number of women becoming mothers outside matrimony and in Britain today a quarter of all children are born to unmarried mothers. This is indicative of significant changes in the way in which women's fertility outside marriage is treated. Pregnancy is no longer such a strong prompt to marriage and substantially fewer children born outside marriage are given up for adoption. Single-parenthood should not, however, be necessarily associated with lone-parenthood as the trend marks an increasing reluctance to marry existent partners. With the rise in numbers of children born outside marriage since the 1960s, there has also been a steady increase in the proportion of extra-marital births registered by both parents to reach 70 per cent in 1988 (OPCS, 1989) of whom 7 out of 10 share a common address. From this it has been argued that the majority of children born outside marriage are the products of a relatively stable union between parents. Of those remaining, although they are single mothers, a third share a household with their own parents and others will be living with fresh partners. Hence both divorce and unmarried motherhood relate to, but are not coterminous with, single parenting.

The biggest increases in lone parenthood are found in Britain and the USA. 'In 1986, of all the families containing dependent children, one in seven was a one-parent family, and nine out of every ten one-parent families was headed by a lone mother' (Haskey, 1989). This compares with one in twelve in 1971. In the USA, Glick (1979) has estimated that by the year 1990 a quarter of children under eighteen will be living in single-parent households. Nevertheless, Haskey (ibid) also suggests that these figures contain some uncertainty, as estimates of lone mothers include mothers who are not alone, but cohabiting, and mothers married but living alone.

However, emphasis on the instability of marriage, the rise of cohabitation and the number of children born outside marriage betrays an ignorance of our familial past. The work of historians and historical demographers (Laslett, 1977; Stone, 1977, Macfarlane, 1986) have noted the fluctuating rates of illegitimacy in the past and Anderson (1983) has warned against the development of false nostalgia for some lost golden age of family life; a third of marriages entered into in 1860 ended within twenty years, a figure remarkably comparable with today's proportion, although the reason for past instability was death rather than divorce. The preference for marriage not only has a chequered history it also has an uneven distribution within Western society, with cohabitation being a long-established part of Scandinavian and Caribbean culture. The rise in cohabitation and divorce may be seen as symptomatic of the move away from traditional conceptions of marriage and towards relationships of what Lasch (1977) termed 'non-binding commitment'. Here cohabitation may not be the antithesis of marriage but its logical extension, with its emphasis on the personal and the private, reflecting a growth in individualism and a desire to place relationships outside the church and the state. In statistical terms and official records divorce and cohabitation trade against one another as the growth of cohabitation depresses the divorce rate.

In this debate there are differences of emphasis. The picture varies between whether it is households or individuals that are being examined. At the household level, a quarter contain one person and 8 per cent are lone-parent households. When individuals are the focus of analysis, the significance of the married couple increases, as nearly eight out of ten people in private households live in one formed around a married couple or a couple living as married. Despite familial change there remain strong continuities of domestic partnership in family life. Also there are differences of emphasis in the interpretation of indices. Chester's demographic description of the neo-conventional family (1985) reasserts the continuing importance of marriage and couple-based households by statistical emphasis. He argues that although the proportions of households conforming to the conventional pattern of married couple with dependent children has fallen, most people will spend at least part of their childhood within such a family and go on to form similar households as adults. The issue is, then, not that a third of first marriages fail, but that two-thirds survive. One could move from the statistical optimism of Chester to the stance of many feminists, where the problem is not the growing instability of marriage but its continued survival in a modern world.

Today the divergence of black and white marriage patterns appears to be considerable on both sides of the Atlantic. In the USA substantially lower proportions of black women marry than their white counterparts and the gap is growing. Bennett, Bloom and Craig (1989) estimate that 9 per cent of white women born in the 1950s will remain unmarried, whereas the figure for black women in this age cohort has risen to 31 per cent. They suggest that black marriage rates have declined because of fewer available men, the growing poverty of the black underclass which undermines conventional marriage, and the role of out-of-wedlock child-bearing. A woman with children may not see the necessity for marriage or, in the context of economic hardship, may be seen as a greater burden in marriage. Ethnic differences in British marriage patterns are glimpsed in the figures for single-parenting. In 1984 42 per cent of families with dependent children, of West Indian or Guyanese origin, were headed by a single parent. This contrasts with the 11 per cent of white families and 4 per cent of Asian families which were headed by a single parent (National Council for One Parent Families, 1987).

So far the discussion has concentrated on the West, but Moore's survey (1988) of the anthropological literature on women notes a more global change. This change is not towards a simple Westernisation and acceptance of a 'nuclear' form, although a number of the changes bear its features – greater choice in spouse selection, greater independence for the married couple, more emphasis on love and companionship, a preference for monogamy, and increased divorce. In family life, as elsewhere, the impact of Western thought is mediated by economic change and local culture. 'Modernisation' in the Third World has meant migration, especially for men, the feminisation of subsistence agriculture, and rapid urbanisation. The developing climate of economic individualism has brought fresh permutations to reliance on kin and husband, and in Africa and South America there has been an increase in the numbers of female-headed households and in the numbers of women choosing not to marry. For Moore, ' "nuclearization" is one strategy among several [and] . . . not a strategy open to all. The poor, the single, the widowed and others cannot afford to abandon the "web of kinship" which provides their safety net' (ibid, p. 135). In this way economic change has brought diversity and individualism, and variability in marriage patterns.

Moore's discussion of the Third World has a relevance closer to home. The present model of 'the family' was fashioned by the middle classes in the eighteenth and nineteenth centuries and supported by the organised working class in their claim for a family wage. However, there was always a difference between this model and the actual structures of households in which people lived. The attractions of marriage are relative to the social class position of men and women, and working-class women in the past relied on kin ties and other women for their survival as much as on their husbands (Ross, 1983). Class culture and household resources made their relationship with any husband qualitatively different.

Conclusion

Marriage is important in all women's lives, whether they are married or not. In the symbolic representation of women the qualities of wife and woman are interlinked and the gendering of women in their public and private lives becomes a single whole. On a more material level welfare policy may privilege the married and both compensate and police the non-married, and the structure of the female labour market contains the assumption that working women are married. Also the couple is the essential unit of household organisation and domestic economy for adults who do not live alone. No woman escapes its influence.

There is no clear divide between marriage and non-marriage and there are varying degrees and states of non-marriage. There are never-married women who cohabit and single women who have been married, as well as married women who do not regularly live with their husbands. These women who occupy the margins of marriage are the focus of the book. They are a group growing in numerical importance, given the changing pattern of marriage, and one that presents problems for welfare policies. They are also a group that has been neglected in analyses of 'the family' or divided and examined in particular problem categories. This book is, then, an attempt to redress omissions and misrepresentations, and the next chapter takes a closer look at particular examples of women who are marginal to marriage.

2

Women and the margins of marriage

The discussion in the previous chapter has provided an overview of contemporary changes in the pattern of marriage. Like most discussions of the area it draws largely on a conventional classification of women by marital status which divides them into the single, the married, the widowed, the separated and the divorced. These latter groups are important examples of women without husbands, but there are many women whose marital and quasi-marital experiences are more elastic and, if analysis turns to relationships rather than status, many more women hover at the edge of marriage. As well as women whose marriages have dissolved through death or divorce, there are those who are separated because of employment or because husbands are detained in custody, and women in consensual unions, who live with a partner or who have stable, visiting relationships. In this perspective marriage is a question of degree, stretching from those outside marriage, to those partially married, to those conventionally married. The discussion of these examples links to discussion of conventional marriage, its structure, its normality and popularity. They are part of a single familial system, ordering domestic relationships and economic and social support, constructing sexuality, caring for children and establishing kinship ties. But a conceptual framework which sees them as the other side of the same coin would be false, as these variations exist under the dominant influence of conventional marriage.

Differences do exist between women without husbands and these relate to a number of factors. First, the nature of their marital status and domestic relationships gives a different emotional tone to the particular circumstances of a lone wife. Death and divorce are frequently compared and contrasted. Divorce results from a decision, is fraught with personal antagonism and accompanied by feelings of failure and/or betrayal. A divorced woman may continue a relationship with an ex-husband and this is especially so when there are children. Bereavement permits women to remember their lost marriages more positively and these are more likely to be idealised as they are reconstructed in and through memories. Becoming a widow is less of a political issue amongst children, kin and friends and produces fewer tugs of loyalty, more rallying round and less embarrassment. Also death is accompanied by rituals, where grieving can be more open. Second, marital ties not only change and loosen in dissolution, they also may not be fully formed. Here cohabitation is seen as an alternative to marriage or an unofficial marital form. Alternatively marriages may be legally formed, but a peripheral part of the daily lives of women. This introduces the least visible group, and perhaps the most anomalous, women who are married but, through force of circumstance, not living with their husbands.

Throughout, there are different implications for relationships with new and former partners, and in drawing the continuum there are assumptions about levels of marriage. These degrees of marriage vary with age, class and ethnicity, factors which influence the experiences of women and others' perception of them. As the different groups of women without husbands are keyed into social structure, so their collective features change. The following discussion focuses on the differences between women without husbands, whereas subsequent chapters deal with the common threads in their lives. It explores some examples of women without husbands, starting with those with less connection to marriage – widows – and moving towards women with increasingly stronger connections to marriage.

The widowed

In earlier centuries in the Western world widows dominated the category of women without husbands and death was a major source of instability in marriage. Macfarlane (1986) estimates that, from medieval times to the mid nineteenth century, about half of those who married in their mid-twenties had lost their partner before they reached sixty, and Anderson (1983) suggests that marriages in the last century were as fragile as those today: in the 1860s a third of all marriages dissolved with the death of a partner within twenty years of being formed.

Widows are seen as an historically vulnerable group, but their position in socio-economic structures has been very varied. It depended on how far they were absorbed into wider kin groups and the extent to which they controlled the means of their own economic survival. This reflected the place of women in the economy and in kinship networks, and their right to inherit from their husbands. In agrarian economies, where marriage was intrinsic to the control of resources, widowhood was not just a problem of personal loss, it threatened to alter economic connections and undermine the authority of kin groups. There have been a number of historic solutions to the problem of widowhood and three very different ones are described below.

One solution was the levirate or 'widow inheritance'. This is often interpreted as a woman marrying her husband's brother, but it would be more accurate to say that she remained married to her husband through his brother and could continue to procreate children on behalf of the dead man. This solution was historically widespread and the most quoted examples are found in Ancient Judaism and India. Here the problem of widowhood is resolved by the full and continuing absorption of the woman into her husband's kin group and widowhood as a social category is abolished. Evans Pritchard encountered similar assumptions amongst the Nuer (1990). They had no concept of widowhood, since the rights of marriage and kinship connections were indissoluble and unaltered by death. In Nuer society women could also be married by proxy to the ghosts of dead men.

An equally radical solution to widowhood was also found in India, but this was one of exclusion rather than absorption. Hindu women in the custom of *sati* or 'suttee' were obliged to commit suicide on the funeral pyres of their dead husbands. There are a number of explanations for this practice. *Sati* has an economic basis. It was customary in India for a husband's property to be equally distributed between his mother and his sons. There was no place for the widow and she had no independent means. As marriage had severed the ties with her own family and her husband's family would not support her, the only option was suicide. However, economic explanations are equivocal, since Bayly (1981) notes that *sati* rates were higher in Bengal, an area where widows had more rights to inherit a husband's property and where, he argues, there was stronger religious pressure towards suicide.

Simple economic explanations are then limited as *sati* is also a religious act.

Sati is related to Hindu culture and the caste system. It is an act of self-sacrifice to assist the spiritual progress of the husband after death and it was practised more by higher caste women. In Hinduism, religious status is dependent on the strict observation of rituals which prevent the pollution of individuals and the household. 'Since a widow was perceived almost literally to be part of her husband's body, her presence in a household raised questions of pollution . . . [Hence] the highest castes would only tolerate a widow who practises extreme asceticism' (ibid, p. 175). The higher the woman's caste, the more dependent they were on their families, the greater their seclusion, the stronger the prohibition on divorce and the greater the pressure towards *sati*. Patterns of upward mobility in India have involved the processes of 'sanskritanisation' as groups imitate the dietary restrictions and the increased seclusion and dependence of women in marriage found among higher castes. As sanskritisation spreads in contemporary India, more widows are encouraged to enter perpetual mourning.

Medieval England provides a third example of the variable economic and social status of widows. Here a widow was entitled under common law to a third of her husband's freehold estate (the dower), although Hanawalt (1986) argues that she frequently received more in his will. For Hanawalt the status of the medieval widow was a continuation of the independence of the conjugal household after the death of a spouse and an extension of the mutuality of marriage, as widows were frequently the executors of their husbands' wills. They often continued the land tenancy of their husbands, and where they did not it was expected that sons would make provision. Analysis of manorial court records contains evidence of widows buying land, pursuing trades and arranging the marriages of their children. Here widowhood was associated with greater freedom and independence, and among those who remarried there was less parental pressure in the choice of their new partner. This was the historic position of women married to tenant farmers, yeomen and craftsmen while, among the poor, circumstances were less secure. However, with the development of a more modern economy, where day and wage labour were common and the role of women became more confined to the household, the position of widows not only changed, but worsened.

The independence of widows in the West influenced their cultural identity. Jokes, proverbs and homilies contained images of comfortable and merry widows. However much the virginity of the nubile and innocent maiden might be relished, marriage to a widow was seen to have its compensations, as they were valued for their sexual experience, their domestic skills, their less demanding natures and their retention of their husband's assets. Nevertheless widowhood was associated with deprivation and grief, and also stigmatised. Widows are women tainted by an aura of death. In medieval Europe they were seen as the carriers of ill-omen and frequently accused of being involved in witchcraft and satanic practices. In contemporary Western society, elderly widows may be pitied more than feared, but they remain a margin-alised group. Fennell, Phillipson and Evers (1988) argue that they suffer ageism and sexism and are seen as both unattractive and unproductive.

In contemporary society, death of a spouse is associated with old age, and though couples in the companionate marriage may hope to die at the same time, it is usually the woman who is left. Here Britain is representative of other Western nations: 14 per cent of women over 16 are widows, compared to 4 per cent of men over 16. Furthermore, over a third of women aged 65–74 and nearly two-thirds of those over 75 are widows (*Social Trends*, 1989). This reflects the increased life expectancy of women, their tendency to marry older men and the fact that widowers marry more frequently and more quickly after bereavement.

Widowhood has been incorporated into the contemporary model of the female life-cycle. Hareven (1982), in her exploration of New England kinship structures at the turn of the century, described how for women beyond fifty widowhood signalled the onset of old age. Younger widows were more likely to continue as heads of households, often with the assistance of resident kin, but after 50, such independence became more untenable. She argues that 'The greater propensity of older women to live with kin reflects an overall tendency in the society to shelter women in family arrangements rather than have them live with strangers . . . This practice was both protective and utilitarian – young and old, unattached women often contributed to housekeeping and child care' (p. 176). Hareven comments that the 'empty nest' household was a rarity in the New England community, because women were widowed earlier and it was customary for at least one adult child to then remain at home to care for ageing parents.

Today the situation is different. Characteristically, children will have left home for a number of years prior to a wife's bereavement and this colours the associations of widowhood. It is seen as a natural end to women's lives and, being associated with ageing, it relates to the loss of social contact and the closure of the social world. Loneliness is a major problem in old age and social isolation especially marked in those stranded at home by ill-health and lack of transport. Bowling and Cartwright identify widows' most pressing practical problems as 'adapting to living alone, coping with new household tasks, and the adjusting to a new lower income' (1982, p. 91). Also there are the painful adjustments to learning to shop and cook just for one. In the Bowling and Cartwright study, although many widows moved in the months following their husband's death, there was a reluctance to relinquish their independence by moving in with friends or relatives. The trauma of bereavement and contingent isolation increase the likelihood of widows suffering from mental health problems and physical illness. Here the discussion of widowhood merges with the wider debate on the problems of caring for and supporting the elderly.

The divorced and the separated

Divorce and separation are distinct marital statuses, although separation is seen as a half-way house, part of the dynamics of marriage or a prelude to divorce. It is estimated that between 40 per cent and 50 per cent of couples who separate become reconciled. But this reconciliation is often only temporary, a rehearsal for a later and more permanent dissolution of marriage. Historically the categories were connected as the divorced had only limited rights to remarry and the commonest form of divorce was more akin to a judicial separation. Also divorced and separated couples may have frequent contact with one another, making the dissolution of marriage less complete.

For Delphy (1984) divorce was traditionally marriage in another form, where a wife's entitlement to support for herself and her children was matched by her continuing responsibility for childcare. Ahrons and Rodgers (1987) examine the amount of contact between divorced and separated couples. They found connections especially strong when children were present, but the links were not necessarily dependent on this. Their study describes how individuals may live in single-parent households but have multi-parenting relationships. However it is an approach that is devoid of gender politics. By contrast the contributors to Smart and Sevenhuijsen's collection of papers on child custody (1989) root their analyses of the reformulation of parental rights and responsibilities after divorce in the distribution of gendered power in the family.

In societies where children are incorporated into the mother's lineage there tends to be a more tolerant attitude towards divorce. Also the marriage pattern of historic Europe had, unlike most other parts of the world, been based on monogamy, and in Roman and early Germanic society monogamy was accompanied by easy divorce. With the development and the spread of Christianity from the tenth century onwards, the church struggled to control matrimony, and divorce was made progressively more difficult. Ariès (1985) does not see the religious pressure for indissoluble marriage as going against the communal grain. The material interests of peasant and aristocratic families required that marital arrangements be 'definitive and irrevocable' (p. 144). Marriage was now not only to one person, but for life.

In church thinking the strict regulation of sexuality through marriage was the secular compromise for those who could not aspire to the higher state of celibacy. In modern parlance the church forbade divorce with the right to remarry, but marriages could be nullified and judicial separations were available from the ecclesiastical courts. In the medieval church quasi-divorce was available in two forms. A couple could seek release from the chains of marriage, divorce *a vinculo*, on the grounds that the marriage was legally improper in the first instance. An application for an annulment could be made on many grounds: for example that one of the parties was coerced, that they had already established a relationship with another person or that they were related – the church forbade marriage between relatives closer than seventh cousins. However, there was a penalty for women in divorce *a vinculo*, as, if the marriage was deemed never to have existed, women lost all rights to inheritance and claims to support. Marriages could also be ended *a mensa et thoro*, literally from bed and board. This form of divorce was equivalent to a judicial separation, where there was no possibility of remarriage and the wife was entitled to alimony. Her economic rights in marriage were not lost but she remained a legal minor under the control of her husband.

The Protestant Reformation brought little change. Despite the greater stress on individual conscience and an initial willingness to see marriage as a contract rather than a sacrament, the rules permitting divorce became more stringent as many of the earlier grounds for annulment were now removed. The routes out of marriage narrowed and for those who wanted more than a separation the only official escape became divorce by Act of Parliament. This was the prerogative of the very rich and of men, and was accompanied by the strengthening rights of fathers to the unchallenged custody of their children. The poor resorted to unsanctioned ways around the law. There were more common-law and clandestine marriages and 'wife-sales' (Menefee, 1981), where an unwanted wife would be auctioned in a public place often to a prearranged highest bidder. But in all this it was the middle income groups who had no respectable or affordable way out.

In the mid nineteenth century civil authorities took jurisdiction over marriage and divorce, but they largely absorbed existent ecclesiastical assumptions. Divorce remained difficult, expensive and more available to men. Its limited availability was based on the doctrine of matrimonial offence and guilty party, and the rules contained double standards. Adultery was sufficient grounds for husbands to divorce wives but adultery aggravated by other matrimonial misdemeanours, such as cruelty and desertion, was necessary for wives to be able to petition, should they be able to afford litigation. The state had become the agent for the imposition of the morality of the church. There was to be no collusion in the proceedings and divorce was structured in the courts as adversarial. At this time the courts primarily ruled on whether a marriage should or should not be permitted to dissolve and not on the consequences of its dissolution for the care and control of children or the division of economic assets.

Fletcher (1988a) argues that the liberalisation of divorce was part of a wave of law reform which aimed to enhance individual freedom. Mount (1982) sees the trend as recovering the control of relationships from both state and church and placing it where it belongs, in the hands of individuals. The change in the perception of divorce can be related to changing attitudes towards marriage. As marriage was seen as a personal preserve, a private relationship, it became more untenable for the state to maintain it as an indissoluble union. There was concern about the illicit unions of those unable to obtain a divorce, a surge of sympathy for couples trapped in bad marriages and a desire to free children from the trauma of living in an unhappy home. As marriages became psychologised and individualised, divorce became easier and remarriage seen as a lesser evil than illicit union.

Divorced women are a growing sector of the population: one in twenty women are divorced, a proportion slightly higher than that for men. Although a quarter of all marriages currently formed will end in divorce, high remarriage rates produce a rapid turnover in the populations of both the married and the divorced. In recent years the gap between first marriage and divorce has been narrowing – for those marrying in the late 1970s 17 per cent of women under thirty were separated within six years of their first marriage, compared with 6 per cent of those married in the early 1960s (OPCS, 1989). Three-quarters of all women divorced in the 1970s were remarried within six years and at current rates half of these will again divorce. The pattern is also strongly influenced by age and class. For women married in the late 1970s, a quarter of those under twenty had separated within six years, a figure which drops to less than one in ten for women married in their late twenties. The chances of divorce are further increased when husbands are also in their teens. Low income, economic insecurity and material deprivation combine with early marriage to undermine the stability of marriage, to magnify disadvantage. Not only is the incidence of divorce mediated by class, but so are its consequences. Here the growth of divorce has been linked to housing problems and the feminisation of poverty (see Chapter 6).

Outside these variations there are a number of key features of contemporary divorce, which, in varying degrees, characterise the western world. These changes have altered the operations of the courts, the bases of legal argument between men and women and the experience and aftermath of divorce. First, legislation which introduced no-fault divorce has meant that divorce is obtained on the grounds of irretrievable breakdown and irreconcilable differ-ence. Many of the indices of irretrievable breakdown are comparable to older matrimonial offences, but the legislation has given a different tenor to the proceedings and made divorce cheaper and more accessible to middle income groups. The court is now rarely deciding if a marriage shall or shall not be dissolved, as no undefended case is rejected and few defences are upheld. As collusion is no longer outlawed, petitioners are more inclined to select non-adversarial grounds and petitions are toned down so as not to provoke hostility. Today, many divorces are paper transactions, with the court having a mainly administrative function and Burgoyne, Ormrod and Richards (1987) argue that it is now just a short step from the present proceedings to the court merely being informed that a marriage has been dissolved on a particular date. In recent years wives have been the most likely to petition for divorce and in Britain over 70 per cent of petitioners are women, but there is some suggestion from the USA that the change to a no-fault system has been accompanied by more men filing for divorce. However, the concept of no fault applies more to men than women, since conduct in marriage will be ignored only when there is agreement over the financial settlement and the custody of children, and insofar as it is considered 'equitable' to do so. In practical terms faithless wives do not have the same right to family assets as faithful and blameless ones.

Second, the intervention of the court is now primarily concerned with the distribution of property in marriage and the care and custody of children, whereas in earlier times these matters were more peripheral. Bahr (1983) has suggested that the move towards no-fault divorce has weakened the bargaining power of women, who in the past could use their opposition to divorce to increase the level of the settlement. Consent has lost its leverage, since one partner can no longer block the dissolution of marriage, but divorce without fault or offence has done little to diminish the hostility between divorcing partners. There are still clashes of interest in the financial settlement and this, together with the visitation pattern, provides avenues for hatred and antagonism stirred in the break-up.

Third, no-fault divorce has been accompanied by the adoption of new principles in divorce settlement which relate to the division of property and the claims for continued maintenance. The unpaid contribution that women make to the family and household has been increasingly recognised and reflected in the 'equitable' distribution of family assets and community property. However, equitable means fair rather than equal and alters little in a gendered interpretation of marriage and its dissolution. There is court discretion in what is defined as equitable and this has not always worked to the benefit of women. Smart's study (1984) of solicitors' perceptions and assumptions shows that, whatever their professional appreciation of changes in the law, they have considerable sympathy for the husband and a conventional and traditional view of the division of domestic labour, where women are primarily dependants and not contributors. It is not always clear what is a family asset and what constitutes community property. Does it include objects, the matrimonial home, other property, pension and social security rights and business assets? There are similar problems with family liabilities. These changes have led to the restructuring of arguments, not their abolition. For those with significant amounts of property, the preparation for a divorce may begin with men hiding family assets and women hiring financial detectives.

Women's greater participation in paid employment has led them to be considered economically self-sufficient and lessened their claim to continued financial support from former husbands. The emphasis on assets has replaced that on alimony and there is a widespread desire, wherever possible, for divorce to produce a clean financial break from marriage. Apart from maintenance for children there are fewer lingering financial ties between divorcees – in the United States 14 per cent of divorcees obtain alimony and where it is paid in Britain amounts are small and 'rehabilitative', paid until wives can support themselves. There are suggestions that this has resulted in the long-term financial disadvantage of women, an issue more fully discussed in Chapter 6.

The changes in divorce have also been accompanied by changes in the awards of child custody. In earlier centuries the power of men in marriage over women and children meant that men gained custody and children were regarded as part of their property. In the post-war years the thinking about, and treatment of, children in divorce has changed. Under the influence of developmental psychology, children are seen to need their mothers more and, in tune with the more child-centred approach to families, divorce is seen as a problem because it traumatises children. The move has been away from the rights of the father towards the best interests of the child, and the best interests of the child have in recent years been interpreted as children remaining with their mothers. Women, as a result, are now awarded custody of children in 90 per cent of cases and their rights to custody are largely unchallenged for younger children and girls. Today however there have been fresh developments in the interpretation of the best interests of the child and joint custody settlements are more favoured, in an effort to maintain the continued co-parenting of children, despite the dissolution of marriage. This is again in response to reports of the deleterious effects on children of the severing of ties with the absent parent, usually the father, and the strength of pressure groups, such as Families Need Fathers. Although in financial terms divorce may mark a cleaner break than ever before between the partners, where children are involved there are stronger pressures to continue co-parental responsibilities. This will be more thoroughly discussed in Chapter 8.

A final development has been the growth of a divorce industry, where help is available from a galaxy of professionals offering counselling, therapy, mediation and conciliation in the process. Here divorce is seen as a normal part of the life course and as another developmental task to be accomplished, a circumstance calling for psychic growth and personal adjustment. Such an approach is part of the wider medicalisation of marriage (Morgan, 1985) where human relationships are seen as having disorders which can be eased. The therapeutic approach to divorce is similar to the approach towards marriage as it seeks to foster understanding of the other's viewpoint, to focus on what good feelings remain, to lessen antagonism and to promote co-operation. Marriage guidance and conciliation supports not only a companionate marriage but also a companionate divorce. It is assumed that the capacity for the couple to act in the spirit of the no-fault and non-adversarial divorce is helped by their arrival at court with some settlement in mind and that this depends on their continuing ability to co-operate.

Agreement is often seen as indicative of equity in the arrangement. However, Parkinson (1986) introduces the feminist argument that women are disadvantaged in divorce by the processes of conciliation. The finances of the relationships are largely left to solicitors, since conciliators may find themselves facing charges of negligence if they stray too far into this province. Negotiation and conciliation then concentrate on access to children and here the pressure is for the wife to 'be reasonable'. The changing aspects of divorce relate to the changing assumptions of marriage and all have diverse implications for women.

Women in husband-absent marriages

Many women, at some time or another, find themselves married to a man who is absent from home for a period of time. Intermittent husband absence is not rare and it is associated with a number of occupations, forming part of the life-style of fishermen, long-distance lorry drivers, off-shore oil workers, corporate executives and members of the armed forces. The wives of men working on contract overseas, internal migrants hunting for work and prisoners are further examples of this group. Unlike widowhood and divorce, there is a more obvious continuity with normal marriage and this is a source of different types of contradiction, with women committed to a relationship from which husbands are absent. Also some of the problems of husband absence attach to how it is seen, as much as how it is experienced, and this is indicative of the anomalous status of a wife without a husband.

Gillis notes that in the past itinerant workers established partial marriages with women. Sailors formed customary marriages with 'sailors' wives', 'drawing his half-pay while he was at sea and looking after him while in port' (1985, p. 201). Canal and railway navvies took temporary 'wives' as they moved between jobs. Absence and migration encouraged these short-term relationships but for those women who were formally married it created a marital limbo.

Husband absence is related to the growth of economic individualism and here its most dramatic effects are seen in the Third World. Moore (1988) identifies migratory labour and its contingent pattern of husband absence as one of the main processes underlying present trends towards the feminisation of subsistence agriculture. As men move off in search of work or concentrate on cash crops, women in the Third World are left to provide for the family needs, which they may supplement with petty trading and wage labour. As Tinker argues, 'Statistics show that one-third of farm managers in Africa south of the Sahara are women, with even higher percentages recorded on some countries: 54 per cent in Tanzania and 41 per cent in Ghana' (1981, p. 60). The bulk of these are women with absent husbands.

Married couples today are assumed to be co-resident, but when one partner is away this is characteristically the man. Clark *et al* sees husband absence as an extension of a traditional division of labour in the home. 'Are not *all* husbands intermittently absent . . . [since a] "typical" family regime is one in which the father is absent from home, children and spouse for considerable periods of the day or week for rest, sleep and domestic service' (1985, p. 46). The absence of a husband may be a frequent occurrence or rare, for short or lengthy periods of time, but when it happens women find themselves in the situation of being lone wives. Such a situation receives little or no formal recognition and the impact on the marriage remains largely invisible. It does not attract the interest of the state, as the obligations between husband and wife remain intact. However, many of these women face circumstances similar to those firmly and formally outside marriage.

Husband absence is rarely seen as the husband's problem. He is a free quasi-single individual whereas she is essentially dependent and domestic. For him, absence from home may be sad or exciting, but his reactions are essentially superficial and idiosyncratic. By contrast wives left without the daily presence of a husband are in a type of marriage which is seen as abnormal and stressful. Despite the feminist critique of normal marriage, husband absence is not seen to offer women opportunities. The empirical search has been for psychological disorder and disrupted patterns of eating and sleeping among wives, as well as emotional disturbance among their children, and assessments of how well they cope with their unnatural home circumstances.

As husband absence is more than a problem of women's psychology it is helpful to discuss it within the context of women's marital and other careers. A study of women married to naval personnel in Britain (Chandler, 1989) demonstrates how the experience of husband absence is shaped by a commitment to normal marriage and interconnected with housing patterns and marriage career. The wives of naval ratings marry young, encouraged by service regulations that tie access to the cheap accommodation of service housing to matrimony. Living together in privately rented accommodation does not make financial sense and marriage strengthens personal commitment in the face of frequent service separation. Young wives characteristically move away from home communities to be 'with' their husbands and his going to sea is ironically often a prompt to marriage. Many young wives, on marriage, find themselves living in a distant part of the country, away from family and friends and with a husband at sea. Many find the early separation traumatic as the desire to marry overrides any awareness of the problems this might generate. Women living in service accommodation have difficulty in finding work, as estates are often situated away from centres of employment and employers are reluctant to offer jobs to women mobile with the changing drafts of their husband. With husbands away, in an initially strange community and without work, women often experience a crushing sense of lonelines and meaninglessness. A common solution to the problem is to have a baby, in the hope that their time will be fuller and their days become more meaningful. Motherhood validates them as wives in a way that this type of marriage cannot and a baby provides an entry into the social life of the estate and friendship groups with other women. These groups are intense and child-centred, and they provide opportunities for daily contact, opportunities which many women take, so long as their husbands are away.

Women in maturer marriages move from the naval estate into private housing, driven by the desire not to miss the home-ownership boat, and, as they move, their experience of husband absence changes. First, the problems of buying and selling houses and concern for children's education mean that they are no longer prepared to follow their husbands' drafts. Their more settled existence entails more husband absence, as the weekend marriage, when he is working at a distant shore establishment, is added to the longer separations of sea service. Second, the more experienced naval wives become used to being on their own, to running the house single-handed and around a timetable which suits themselves and the children, and to making all the domestic decisions. This changes the problem of husband absence. Instead of the devastation of being left, women now have the task of reintegrating husbands into the household and coping with the irritation of changing household routines. Throughout, the experience of husband absence is mediated by class. Officers' wives are women who have married later, are more likely to have their own careers and access to greater resources. As such they fare better in husband absence. They also adopt middle-class ways of making and keeping friends and are more likely to be involved in public, organised activities.

Although the issues of sea service and 'weekending' are the same for all women, the context and the approach to them are varied.

Women in consensual unions

Where women are cohabiting with partners or have a stable visiting relationship, the debate moves closer still to marriage. Although living together is often regarded as a form of unofficial marriage, the distinction between cohabitation and marriage is culturally specific, part of the dialogue between state law, religious authority and custom. Comparative analysis of marriage customs finds little commonality other than the public recognition of a relationship and this blurs any distinction between marriage and cohabitation. Marriage may be recognised in elaborate ritual and religious sanctification or relate to administration procedures as in the kibbutz, where the marriage of the couple may be recognised when they apply for joint accommodation. In the West, where consensual unions are distinguished from marriage, they are linked with illicit sexuality, 'illegitimacy', loose living and an absence of kinship control. Viewed with Western ethnocentricism and legalism, and in the light of church morality, consensual unions are problematised as unstable and immoral.

Furthermore, the bundle of rights with which marriage is associated in the West – exclusive sexual access, paternity of children, co-residence and a shared domestic economy – may not be found together in 'marriages' elsewhere. This has led some anthropologists to shy away from any use of the word 'marriage'. As Needham says, ' "Marriage" is an odd-job word: very handy in all sorts of descriptive sentences, but worse than misleading in comparison and no real use at all in analysis' (Needham, 1971, pp. 7–8). The distinction is also unclear in people's public definitions of themselves. In the General Household Survey in Britain, 70 per cent of those cohabiting at the time of the interview at first declared themselves to be married (OPCS). The legal distinction between children born in and out of wedlock has been eroded or abolished and the numbers of children born to unmarried parents has steadily climbed to reach 20 per cent in the USA, 25 per cent in Britain and 45 per cent in Sweden. However here we run into definitional problems again, as being born to an unmarried parent does not mean being born into a single-parent household, as many of the women who have children may be in relatively stable relationships.

However, cohabitation may not be a single phenomenon as people cohabit for different reasons. Trost (1985) identified two types of cohabitation in nineteenth-century Sweden which were linked to class culture. There were bourgeois couples who had a conscientious objection to the religious control of marriage. By contrast, among the poor, and especially the migrants seeking work in a growing industrial economy, marriage was rejected not through principle but because the couple were insufficiently well-off to establish and sustain a durable household.

This historical distinction is also relevant today. There is no easy terminology for the cohabiting, but perhaps the commonest term, especially in bourgeois cohabitation, is 'partner'. Although this has a contractual connotation it does sum the more limited nature of the relationship. Bourgeois cohabitation is an extension of bourgeois marriage, with its ideological emphasis on individualism and privacy, especially from the state and wider kin. Trost (1985) argues that cohabitation in Sweden furthers the society of couples. Here it relates to affluence, the greater adaptability of work regimes to the familial responsibilities of men and women, where women have been more involved in paid employment and men are assumed to have more responsibilities in childcare and the home, and to a welfare system not devised to economically punish unmarried mothers. Cohabitation among the poor may not attract the same ideation, as in blue-collar marriage it is linked to material survival and economic security. Other classifications make similar distinctions (Macklin, 1983; Sarantakos, 1984) stressing the variable range of commitment partners have to each other and the differing expectations about whether they will ultimately marry. Cohabitation then varies from a *de facto* domestic relationship to a commitment encased in a liberal theory of human relationships.

This raises the question of the extent to which cohabitation is experienced as marriage. Cohabitants seem as satisfied with, and as sexually active in, their relationships as married couples (Cotton, Anthill and Cunningham, 1983), though some have a shorter-term perspective on their relationship. Most research suggests that cohabitation does little to alter the sexual division of labour in the home, especially if the couple regard themselves as married. It receives some legitimacy as a trial for the more serious business of marriage. This may be part of its ideology, but there is no indication that prior cohabitation makes for more 'effective' or stable marriages. The identities of husbands and wives are powerful scripts for cohabitants to unlearn. Where cohabitation does make a difference is when the relationship breaks down. The legal proceedings are more difficult and more costly, for before division can be considered, it is first necessary to establish what the rights and relationships were.

Fletcher (1988b) suggests that common-law marriage has no legal basis, but Freeman and Lyon (1983) argue that at law the differences between cohabitation and marriage are being steadily eroded in contemporary Britain. They note that today it is extremely difficult to 'escape from marriage by cohabiting' and this is especially so for couples with children. As cohabitants have the outward appearance of the monogamous nuclear family, judges categorise the relationship as that of *de facto* husband and wife. Where illegitimacy has been abolished, the legal obligations between father and child no longer depend on marriage. They then apply the principles of family law, which stresses the necessity of protecting the economically vulnerable, rather than the principles of contract. Other societies which operate codified rather than common-law systems tend to ignore or penalise non-marital unions. In Sweden the legal status of cohabitants has been given the most explicit consideration. Here, although there is the expressed desire to retain a 'neutrality principle' between marriage and cohabitation, the operations of the law remain confused – the laws of inheritance and property distinguish between marriage and cohabitation, but welfare law treats them as the same.

The extension of marriage to include cohabitation contains problems and dilemmas. The women's movement may wish to see women protected, but not at the expense of abolishing the cohabitation option. There are penalties for women, who may have acted in the partnership as married without having acquired its legal benefits. Perhaps this will be resolved by the establishment of cohabitation contracts, but these may incorporate women into the lives of men without giving them access to resources. In the legal redefinition of 'marriage' as a relationship rather than a status, there is the difficulty of deciding when the relationship is sufficiently close and lasting as to constitute marriage-like cohabitation. Also those changes that have occurred may not remain, as there is opposition to the equation of marriage with cohabitation. Freeman and Lyon comment that this opposition stems from a desire to protect marriage, when what is really under threat is cohabitation.

Despite the difficulties of measuring marital trends, official statistics show steady increases in the numbers of couples cohabiting and children born to unmarried parents. Here it is hard to distinguish life-course issues from social trends. In life-course terms, cohabitation is increasingly the type of relationship formed as a prelude to marriage, and remarriage, and as an aftermath of divorce. However, as the present generation matures the proportion of people in consensual unions may increase, with cohabitation a longer-term option.

The control of marriage has been an historic struggle for the church, which it has not always won. The early evangelising Christian church dismissed existent custom as pagan and tried to control popular morality by matrimony, regulating it through the ecclesiastical and then the secular courts. Religious asceticism had an uneasy relationship with marriage. It was a secular compromise for those unable to aspire to celibacy and in the early days couples were 'married' at the church door, which was more like a priestly blessing for their customary union. In Britain the state did not become involved until 1603, when polygamy became a felony. Gillis (1985) describes the vibrant underworld of unofficial marriage and consensual union in Britain, which the state and the church were never entirely able to suppress. Cohabitation thrived among those who could not afford the expense of the big wedding, among migrant workers and those already married. Local practices of self-marriage and self-divorce flourished and of these the best known are the 'besom marriages'. Couples who were 'living over the brush' had leapt symbolically over a broom crooked in their doorway to signify the start of a common life together. There were also the proletarian practices of 'living tally'. Flandrin (cited in Ariès, 1985) has described similar arrangements in France, where public pledges (*créantailles*) were indicative of little marriages.

In England there were clandestine or 'lawless' marriages, performed without proper bans or parental consent and often by unbeneficed clergymen. The area of the Fleet Prison in eighteenth-century London was notorious for clandestine marriages and was a place where 'marriage houses' retained the services of parsons who performed cheap marriages on demand. They were favoured by couples who wanted to evade parental or parish control, who wanted their reputations protected by some public pledge but within a less binding framework than that of the big wedding. In Britain vestiges of the custom still linger in elopements to Gretna Green. Gillis estimates that clandestine marriages and irregular unions constituted a quarter to a third of all unions in the eighteenth century and a fifth of them at the turn of the nineteenth century.

The church in ancient Sweden also tried to wrest control of marriage away from kinship groups but it was less successful in doing so. Traditionally 'marriage' in Sweden had three elements: the betrothal, the handing over of the bride, and the 'bedding'. In law a betrothal and the establishment of a sexual relationship had the legal status of a partial or 'unfulfilled marriage', the children of which were recognised in law. But even in Scandinavia where cohabitation is well established its rate has in recent years risen. Popenhoe (1987) claims that today Sweden has one of the lowest rates of marriage among industrial societies and the highest average age for first marriages. Swedish women do not get married until they are in their late twenties, and increasingly are not marrying at all. Popenhoe estimates that a quarter of all couples are not married and Trost (1985) argues that since the mid-1960s the marriage rate for women has more than halved. This draws on traditions in Sweden of living together prior to marriage and more relaxed attitudes towards premarital sexual relations. Pejorative descriptions of cohabitations, such as 'living in sin' and 'concubinage', have clear sexual overtones, whereas the more permissive society of Scandinavia stresses its domestic rather than its sexual aspect.

In the above examples cohabitation can be seen to be growing in white western society as a preparation for and a development of white bourgeois marriage and not a radical departure from it. Another major example of consensual union that has a long history is found among Afro-American and Caribbean black families. Studies have shown a range of relationships in this context, where there are visiting and cohabiting unions and women can have 'inside' and 'outside' partners (Smith, 1988; Thorogood, 1987). Smith distinguishes between three types of marriage-like relationships in the West Indies. There are legal unions, common-law marriages and visiting unions, where the men to whom women are married may differ from those with whom they are living and these in turn may differ from the men with whom they are having regular sexual relations.

Explanations of the particular structure of the black family draw on a number of strands in black social history. Jamaican 'illegitimacy' rates have averaged at about two-thirds of all live births since records were first kept in 1870. The 'marriage' patterns of black families result from the interweave of cultural and material factors. The Caribbean was a colonial slave society. Slaves were unable to legally marry and a shifting population of white men employed as managers and book-keepers passed through the islands, forming consensual unions with black women in their often short stays in the colonies. As white men came and went in the Caribbean, women and children formed the core of more stable matrifocal households. Even when slaves were freed, the status gap was too great to permit marriage and hence the black and white population 'mixed without amalgamating' (Smith, 1988) as the women and children were of a different class and status group to the father. Martinez-Alier (1974) quotes the aphorism 'better the mistress of a white man than the wife of a negro' to sum many black women's pragmatic attitude to the colour–class divide. In the dynamics of the colour–class system, 'light' coloured women were always in demand to be the mistresses of white men and these female lines would whiten with the generations. By contrast, men of colour would have to search for partners among the mulatto and black population and these lines would historically darken. In Sweden, living together is a development of coupledom whereas in the Caribbean it is the opposite, where men and women live together because historically they did not form legally and socially recognised couples.

In the late nineteenth century marriage in the West Indies became associated with an urban middle class, with respectability and religious commitment. Consensual unions then became associated with low life and the disorganised poor. But for Smith (1988) non-legal unions are not confined to the poor, but are also a product of inter-class relations. This marriage pattern is not an historic one or one whose principles are confined to the black population as he stresses that all types of union are practised by all groups in Jamaica. It is also not uniquely Creole, but in harmony with other practices throughout the West, where rich men take lower-class women as mistresses and marry only social equals.

Others have traced matrifocality of black families to pre-slavery days. The African heritage left a kinship system that was extensive and female-based and Gutman (1976) has described how this survived despite the dislocation of slavery. Although slaves arrived as individuals, a settled slave society built an increasingly dense network of kinship ties and one that reasserted the links between women. Also Gutman argues that the slave families were often more stable than had been previously supposed, not least of all because it was in the interests of owners to maintain productive and coherent family units. But, as Lebsock (1983) points out, slavery and emancipation had a complex relationship with the family forms of black women. In her study of Petersburg, Virginia, in the early nineteenth century, it is shown that black women had easier access to emancipation than men, and a third of free black women at this time remained single. Lebsock speculates that they may have wished to retain their control over property by avoiding marriage. Also, 'Because blacks were not permitted to marry whites, and slaves were not allowed to marry anyone, the pool of marriageable men was restricted to free blacks, and there were simply not enough of them to go round' (p. 157). And the necessity of consensual union in slave marriage may have remained culturally sufficient for black men and women in emancipation.

In post-slave society the black family has experienced the fresh dislocations of migration as well as the continuing problems of poverty and deprivation. Here racism and economic inequality play a role in the family patterns of a black underclass. Because black men find it hard to obtain well-paid and secure jobs, marriage to them is seen as not guaranteeing material comfort for women and their children. Here the nuclear and patriarchal family may not be the dominant cultural form and, even if it were, it is undermined by poverty and insecurity.

The proportion of common-law or visiting unions increases as analysis moves to the poorer sections of society and younger age groups. Creole society also contains different attitudes towards these domestic arrangements. Consensual unions are more about love and sexual attraction, but marriage is a more practical and serious affair. It is associated with the greater authority of men within the household, a standard of living more dependent on male earnings, greater family ambition and a greater sense of being a couple. Marriage dampens strong views about male unreliability that are frequently held by women who are in consensual relationships. Black marriage patterns link to a domestic economy where men may spread income over several households and women are involved in extensive exchange and help networks. For Smith (1988) the emphasis on marriage blinds analysis to the nature of familial relations where the more organic structures of the West Indian family are flexible around the mother–daughter relationship.

For Gutman and for Lebsock the matrifocality of the black family is seen as a strength and indicative of flexibility in the face of poverty and migration. However not everyone has shared in this interpretation of the nature of black families. Government reports in the United States and Britain have blamed the structure of the black family for the problems of the black community. Black families seen as abnormal and inadequate because women are regarded as ineffectual heads of households, which are seen as more unstable and 'disorganised' than those based on marriage, and because children lack paternal control.

Brittan and Maynard (1984) identify this argument as both sexist and racist, idealising male authority and denigrating black culture. As the white bourgeois family is used as the universal measuring stick, all others fall short and ethnic minorities are problematised in a critique of their family forms. As black women are seen as insufficiently married so Asian women are seen as over-married, overtly dominated by authoritarian fathers and husbands and suppressed by purdah and arranged marriages. They argue that the average suburban white woman does not necessarily have any more personal power than the black woman in a consensual partnership or the Asian women secluded in the wider collectivity of kin. Here there is a bourgeois standard in assessing levels of marriage and bourgeois humbug about the reality of marital relationships. Research often underestimates the levels of resourcefulness and independence of black women and their use of informal community supports. Basic to the black family is the centrality of women in the home and the more tenuous and impermanent presence of men. This links with a more matriarchal structure where, whether women are married or not, they are more emotionally and economically independent of men. Black women see men as less reliable and trustworthy than white women do, and whatever their marital status they can be seen as less married than their white counterparts.

Conclusion

The changing patterns of marriage and familial relationship has meant that today there are large numbers of women living outside marriage or in quasi-married relationships. This chapter has concentrated on the different marital statuses of women and the different relationships to marriage of women who are widowed, divorced, in husband-absent marriage and cohabiting. These categories form a continuum where there are degrees of marriage/non-marriage in the construction and organisation of domestic relationships.

Different historical and cultural contexts have more or less encouraged these relationships and shaped their structure. The social distance between groups and their material circumstances has influenced women's propensity to marry. The rules of kinship obligation, inheritance and property have shaped the treatment of the widowed and the divorced. The labour market and the demands of specific occupations has permitted or discouraged co-residence. Also the cultural definitions of marriage and variable sub-cultural preferences for marriage have influenced the numbers of women who live on its margins and their treatment. Throughout, the incidence and experience of non-marriage and atypical marriage is mediated by class and ethnicity.

However, from these cases a number of more or less common issues emerge from marital loss and dissolution, and from husband/ partner absence. These are issues of access to economic resources, of social and cultural identity and the organisation of personal life. Given the signs of change in married life and a resurgence of interest in 'atypical' family forms, the next issue to be addressed is the significance of these changes. It is necessary to identify appropriate conceptual frameworks within which to discuss the changes and to prompt key questions about the large numbers of women living by choice or force of circumstance on the outskirts of marriage. Feminism has provided theoretical reference points for the examination of the family and these must be fitted to women outside marriage or in atypical relationships as much as to those who are conventionally married. This will provide a better understanding of the variability of family life and a clear conceptualisation of marriage and the family. The next chapter examines the implications of these conceptual frames principally developed for women with husbands, for women who are without husbands.

3

Conceptual themes and issues

The family and marriage today seem beset by contradictions. Although marriage remains popular, with high rates of marriage and remarriage, there is concern that the structure of conventional family life is changing and fears that traditional forms have become unstable and are even in decline. With the rise in divorce, the prevalence of cohabitation and the increasing numbers of single parents, marriage appears to be in abeyance. These fears about the death/decline of the family are an old chestnut of sociological debate. 'The family' is a symbol of social order and any loosening of its patterns of dependence and responsibility fuel anxiety about social disintegration. The distinctions between change and decline are always problematic and political as one person's decadence is another's liberation. However, where it does stir moral panic, the panic focuses primarily on the position of women and the care of children, the familial control of adolescence and the importance of male authority in the household.

One may dispute arguments about decline, but there must be greater recognition of women who live outside marriage or in quasi-marriages. Most women will spend at least some time as women without husbands and many women will spend the bulk of their lives outside conventional marriage. The analysis of their circumstances is important in a number of ways. It contributes to our understanding of the variability of women's lives, whose identities may be deeply influenced by marriage although they live outside it. It will clarify issues in social policy, where past and present domestic relationships shape entitlement and treatment. It also connects to the wider debate on marriage and family form and their relationship to all women's lives.

There is the assumption that marriage is central to the wider reproduction of gender, crucial to the framing of women's private and public lives. As the social aspects of marriage extend beyond the household, wider advantages and disabilities fall on women by virtue of their proximity to it. An analysis of women without husbands is then a continuation of the feminist concern with family life and an attempt to extend its insights beyond conventional family forms to less visible groups, such as elderly widows, and to topics which have proved difficult in feminist theory, such as child custody.

A number of conceptual frameworks are relevant in the elaboration of these issues. An analysis of women without husbands challenges the structures of familism and the connections between kinship and household organisation. It contributes to debates on the distribution of power and its relation to gender and family forms that are found in discussions of patriarchy. It also draws on the different theoretical tradition of the social psychology of women's experience in family life. Here issues of companionship, well-being and personal support are to the fore. It questions how far ostensibly non-married domestic partnerships are like marriage. It provides alternative contexts for the discussion of sexuality and parenting, and a greater sensitivity to the vagaries of female biography. In these discussions there are also issues of 'stock' and 'flow' – the numbers of women with varying marital statuses and in different domestic relationships at any one time and the incidence and frequency of these marital experiences over time and within biography. These are the conceptual starting points for an analysis of women without husbands which derive from a wider sociology of family life and form the theoretical threads that run through subsequent chapters.

Familism

The ideology of 'the family' constitutes it as a private and separate world and one that is the province of women. Here the family in question is nuclear and bourgeois, formed around a homemaker wife and breadwinner husband and their dependent children. But, whatever the ideology, as Morgan (1985) argues, drawing the boundaries of the family is always a way of constituting and understanding the wider world. Although marriage and the family are the epitome of the personal, familistic values penetrate deeply into wider society, with the mythology of privacy merely misting the connections. On close inspection, the penetration of familistic values is visible in many areas: in taxation and property ownership, child custody and maintenance, in medical and welfare services and moral education. Major themes in familism are the aggregation of individuals into families for tax and welfare purposes and as units for consumption and consumerism, and the prioritising of male interests through the dependence of women and children upon men. In this way familism carries gender from the family into wider society, feeding it into the state and into the economy, and simultaneously disadvantaging many women without husbands.

Familism is central to the structure of work and its levels of remuneration. The domestic labour and responsibilities of women limit their participation in paid work. Breaks in employment to care for the elderly and disabled, as well as the care of children, interrupt careers, and the demands of housework and childcare are more easily fitted around part-time employment. These responsibilities weaken the bargaining power of women in the labour market and this is further diminished by the claims of married men and trades unionists for a family wage, sufficient income to support their families and retain the domesticity of their wives. Hence, women's wages and their attitudes to work are trivialised and detached from breadwinning, as their income buys 'little extras' and 'gets them out of the house'. Women's work is also an extension of domestic tasks and women find themselves in male support roles, in cleaning and caring, or doing light assembly work, where female dexterity affords them a gendered suitability. Because of it connections with domesticity, the work of women is diminished, seen as less important than that undertaken by men. Their economic vulnerability is both a cause and a consequence of their dependence on men, as the circular logic that confines women to a secondary position in the labour market and reinforces their economic dependence also supplies the economic grounding for the continuance of marriage. As the logic of familism ensures that marriage remains their best career (Delphy, 1984) it also limits sources of support for women without husbands.

'The family' has a high profile in popular culture. Television thrives on soap operas, with their unending stream of family drama, within dynasties great and small, and situation comedies which poke fun at odd family circumstances. Newspapers rake through the personal lives of the famous for marital misdemeanours, items for public titillation, while also carrying features that seek to take the high moral ground, campaigning for family matters. Here their treatment of the royal family is instructive, caricaturing views on ordinary women. Royal women are criticised for neglecting their babies, for being too fat or too thin, for not being dutiful wives or being wives only out of duty. A different type of family appears in advertising and this is the family of comfortable consumerism, where good wives and good mothers buy the latest products to improve the cleanliness, the health and the care of other members of the household. In this media image 'the family' is a metaphor for everything that is homely and secure, and stands in stark contrast to the public images of the 'broken home' and the loneliness of life without a partner.

Familism shapes the sexual experiences of women and in the West it has been strongly influenced by Christianity. In traditional Christian thinking good women were praised for their modesty and their lack of sensuality, and bad women were castigated as the temptresses of men. Women's sexuality was confined to marriage and subservient to procreation, whereas male sexuality was freer and more self-determining. These gendered differences were reproduced in the developing scientific theories of the nineteenth and twentieth centuries, where men, unlike women, were seen as driven by stronger innate sexual impulses. Both supplied the grounding for the sexual double standard, dividing women into those with unimpeachable and those with easy virtue, women who would be cherished for their modesty and women who would be sexually pursued, overcome and despised. There has been some re-working of sexual attitudes in recent years as liberal Christianity and sexology has incorporated mutual sexual fulfilment and pleasure into companionate marriage. Good women can now enjoy tame domestic sex, but bad women still feature in the passion of 'the affair' or sell their services in recreational sex. And these bad women characteristically live outside conventional marriage.

For a woman reputation remains important. Young girls must use their sexuality to secure a permanent partner, but not appear too available; they must steer a middle course between being frigid and easy, between being a 'slag' and a 'drag' (Lees, 1986). For older women outside marriage, the rules are the same. Their images are those of the dried-up spinster, the man-hungry gay divorcee or the merry widow, the witch, the careerist and the neurotic. As such they are ignored or used by men and feared by married women as man-stealers and marriage-wreckers.

Familism fosters the normality of marriage and general definitions of womanhood rely on its context. As Duquiem argues, 'When women marry, besides placing themselves in a position materially where certain aspects of "feminity" will be difficult to avoid, they have taken one of the major steps towards conforming to the ideology of womanhood' (quoted in Smart, 1984, p. 143). Similarly Oakley (1982) has described how the qualities of all women are entwined with those of wives and mothers. She identifies a complex of traits that go to make a woman and these are passivity, emotionalism, a preoccupation with appearance rather than being, and the nurturing qualities of maternalism. The qualities of a good wife and mother are qualities desirable in all women and central to definitions of the feminine. These qualities are not only seen as desirable but natural and the retreat to naturalism is a measure of their ideological strength. It provides an apparently unchallenge-able basis to the domesticity of women, where maternity links women's true nature to marriage and the family, housecraft and the home. Womanhood ties women to marriage and to men, but an integrative view of traditional womanhood is undermined when its dimensions begin to socially fragment, where maternity is disconnected from wifehood and wifehood is disengaged from co-residence. Here the normality of marriage is threatened not only by the simple numerical fall in those marrying, but also the potential fragmentation of the assumptions of gender. However, familism operates to retain the coherence of gender, the integrity of the family and to problematise women without husbands. This is seen in the cultural definitions of women and in the formulations of state policies.

The relationship between the state and the individual is mediated by assumptions about family life. Zaretsky (1982) argues that ' "the family", in the conventional sense of a private, self-supporting nuclear unit, was to a large extent created by or at least reconstituted by the modern state' (p. 192). Modern family forms are an accommodation to political economy, to a system of wage labour, where independence and flexibility in the living arrange-ments are intrinsic to economic survival. Wage labour operates in a climate of market individualism where the state seeks to guarantee the means by which every family can support itself and steps in only when there is breakdown to institutionalise those without independent means or those without families. This approach has in the past been bolstered by the development of corporate welfare programmes, trade-union protectionism and middle-class philanthropy. But in the last decade corporate solutions to economic problems and welfare issues have lost favour and economic individualism within 'disorganised capitalism' has grown. This has meant more autonomy for women, but some of the reforms that promote the individual rights of women have a negative side and Zaretsky notes the 'costs and limits' for women of 'a society organised around self-reliance, the market and wage labour' (pp. 218–19). These organising principles appear neutral and gender-free, but in their operation they are not.

Poor Law was concerned with kinship liability and the absence of family led to dependence on local and state relief agencies. As a centralised state developed, so did a family policy, prioritising legitimate family life, stepping in only when liable relatives could no longer support individuals, and typically where men had died or absconded from their family responsibility. Paradoxically, divorce legislation also prioritises normal family life (Smart, 1987) by freeing people from failed marriages, permitting previously illicit unions to be recognised and new marriages to begin. However, within the provision there is ambivalence towards women without husbands, ambivalence about whether to treat them as dependants, as mothers caring for the best interests of their children or as workers who should be self-reliant and breadwinning for themselves and their children. There is concern that social security should not make lone parenthood and attractive option and this has created contradictions as the state has not found a way to alleviate the poor, of whom lone women are a substantial part, without condoning non-traditional families.

With the development of welfare services have come family therapists, counsellors and medical practitioners. For Donzelot (1980), these people are 'relational technicians' who police individuals through policing the family. For Morgan (1985) they are part of the medicalisation of family relationships where marital problems are diagnosed and, where possible, repaired in an attempt to avoid family damage. But much of the supervision, counselling and therapy is not directed at women in conventional families, but at women without husbands. Superficially these aforesaid groups appear apolitical but their work is an extension of the cultural imperialism of the bourgeoisie and an attempt to spread their family forms throughout society. They also inhibit the discussion of less conventional ways of organising family life. The intrusion of these technicians into family life has provoked criticism from right-wing individualists on both sides of the Atlantic: Lasch (1977) and Mount (1982) champion the partiarchal family as the natural defender of personal freedom against state interference; but in these discussions the individual always appears to be a man and personal freedom is set in a masculinist mould.

The family is important in the politics of lobbying groups as well as in the activities of health and welfare practitioners and professionals. Berger and Berger (1983) have described 'the war over the family' where the pro-family and pro-life movement grew out of Roman Catholic and fundamentalist support. Its members oppose abortion, pornography, homosexuality and government policies which undermine traditional family values. Abbott and Wallace (1989) describe the family stance of right-wing politics in Britain which simultaneously supports traditional patriarchal families and champions the rights of the individual. In combination these produce contradictions in policies. Traditional families backed by Christian morality and based on mutual support are valued alongside economic liberalism, with its emphasis on the freedom of the individual. Although 'the logical extension of economic liberalism is the fragmentation of the family' (ibid, p. 82), policy statements attempt to elide divergent interests by addressing 'individuals and their families', with the tacit assumptions that individuals are men and families are patriarchal. In policy terms, to appear to be 'the party of the family' has tended to be associated with conservatism and individualism, but all parties claim some affiliation since it is important for image and it guarantees breadth of appeal.

There are some limited points of agreement between the New Right and branches of feminism in emphasising the importance and dignity of what women do and challenging the nature of their easy sexual availability to men. However, the number of points of difference are much greater, and the policies of the pro-family movement have been identified by feminists as contrary to the interests of women. This is exemplified in the debates on abortion and the access of single women to reproductive technologies. Both of these issues have been identified by the New Right as anti-family, as the campaigns value motherhood but wish to locate it firmly in marriage. They also argue for the withdrawal of the state from family affairs, a policy which would make women without independent means more directly the responsibility of men.

The Rapoports (1982) suggest a decline in the social potency of conventional marriage by emphasising the variety and diversity of marital and family forms. They contrast the social tradition and family uniformity of earlier family/community studies with family structures today where there 'is an increased range of options available, . . . not only a greater range of recognised patterns, but an acceptance of the value of enhancing personal freedom to choose the desired pattern' (p. 477). For the Rapoports diversity spells choice and variety for the individual and opportunities to devise their own rules of partnership. But all domestic arrangements are not equal, as all marital forms and types of communal living exist in the shadow of 'conventional families'. This shadow penalises those outside traditional marriage and renders alternative forms odd, inadequate or experimental in nature. Familistic principles may even be extended to incorporate so-called alternatives, as when the rights and obligations of cohabitation are seen as equivalent to those of marriage.

Patriarchy

Patriarchy is a key concept in the analysis of women in all social relationships. Patriarchy is about power and presupposes 'inequality, subordination and dependence' (Gittins, 1985, p. 58) in relations between men and women, in marriage and beyond. Male interests shape sexuality and reproduction, family and household and permeate wider society. Rooted in the family, patriarchy is an organising principle throughout society, where men dominate women and children, and older men dominate younger men. It is also embedded in culture and the psyche, with masculinity expressing the power of the father, and feminity the subordination of women to it. The concept of patriarchy is intrinsic to a feminist critique of society and here it has political objectives as well as analytic value, expressing the oppression and subordination felt by women. It brings hitherto private domestic relations to the foreground of analysis, by focusing on how the processes of production and reproduction intersect. Thus it is an essential tool in exploring the experiences of women with looser domestic connections to men.

Patriarchy has an economic and political content since the domestic relationships of women and their role within reproduction weakens their bargaining position in the labour market, relegates them to a reserve army of labour, confines them to women's jobs and creates their ambiguous relationship with social class. How patriarchy is related to the economy and to capitalism is a contentious area, and there are questions as to whether the oppression of women forms one example of the wider exploitation of workers or whether patriarchy is a distinct and autonomous sphere of exploitation and oppression. Despite the controversies, the concept has a special relevance in the analysis of familial relationships, with its focus on power in patterns of domesticity and reproduction. Here patriarchy challenges 'a more or less straight-forward model of the male breadwinner and the "family wage", and economism . . . [which locates] the central sphere of activity in the public economic sphere, putting to the margin questions of the family, household and sexuality' (Morgan, 1985, p. 220). Although patriarchy is a term which has come to sum all the pervasive inequalities between men and women, its current usage is broader than its original form.

Morgan has attempted to clarify the area by reintroducing the distinction. Originally patriarchy meant 'rule of the father', but its familial grounding is now regarded as only one example of pervasive male power and women's submission to it. It identifies the links between male power and the patriarchal control of property, the cultural centrality of the father figure and the emotional tangles that surround it. This analysis stresses the systematic connection between the power of the father within kinship and wider male domination, which endures in societies where kinship has lost sway as a central organising principle. Morgan wishes to emphasise that men have dominion not just as males but at patriarchs of families, and points to the structural symmetry between father/child and the male/female relationships, the similarities of women's and children's dependency.

Waters (1989) sharpens the distinction in describing changes in the masculine gender system. He suggests that in modern society, as power has moved from the private to the public domain, the system of gender control has also changed. It has moved from 'patriarchy', rule by heads of extended families, to 'viriarchy', rules by adult males, whose power is independent of kinship structures. In developing her model of patriarchy Walby (1990) comes to similar conclusions. She identifies a movement away from patriarchal structures that dominate women through their seclusion in the household to one where women are permitted to participate in the public domain although in a subordinated way. The move to viriarchy or public patriarchy implies that marginality to marriage is more acceptable but it gives women no more autonomy than they had in the past.

However, there is another issue, relevant at a lower level of analysis. Waters is interested in the characterisation of social systems and in particular the nature of the masculine gender system. But Morgan is concerned to stress the dominance of men in households and here patriarchy is central. In households and families men are both fathers and husbands and their relationship with women and children interwoven in a domestic web of male authority. In homes, patriarchy shapes housework, domestic decision-making, sexual regulation, the economic dependence of women and their relationships with children. Here the approach of Walby is again useful. In her analysis of patriarchy sl.ε identifies not a single base but the six patriarchal structures of domestic labour, wage labour, state policy, male violence, sexuality and culture. While not being entirely discrete dimensions they give conceptual clarity to analyses of women without husbands and facilitate more structured analysis. The detachment of women from men may limit domestic labour and domestic violence, but in other areas the rules of patriarchy may be at least as, if not more, stringently applied.

Companionacy

The companionate model of marriage is a thread in post-war and pre-feminist discussions of familial change. The spread of relative affluence, the increased employment of married women, the growth of home-ownership were seen in Britain as the ingredients of home-centredness, conjugal partnership and even marital symmetry. In America the emphasis on companionacy was part of a trend towards psychologising personal relationships, but throughout marital companionacy was seen as an ideal towards which couples strove. Companionacy is then concerned with coupledom, with personal commitment and the privacy of the married. In conceptual terms the emphasis on companionacy is used to deny the social reference points of marriage, as its interpersonal satisfactions and emotional shortcomings are the focus of attention and its institutional bases are of more marginal interest. Its use as a conceptual framework is part of the psychologising of marriage. As marriage is psychologised the interpersonal and the institutional are erroneously counterposed in the assumption that they are alternatives in the structuring of marriage.

Intimacy can however be prescriptive. Mansfield and Collard identify its development in the process of becoming a couple, since 'Once the couple were married it was clear that the brides and grooms expected to relinquish past confidantes and depend mainly, if not exclusively, on their marriage partners' (1988, p. 171). The stress on compatibility and mutual absorption ties couples more firmly together, in an ideal biography, making marriage the kernel of family life and devaluing adult relationships beyond the dyad. As couples are increasingly supposed to turn to their partners for friendship and support, their loss may be so much more devastating. Hence not to be part of a couple is to be lonely and emotionally unsupported.

Berger and Kellner (1980) elevate the assumptions of companionate marriage into a key process in the construction of social order. Marriage is a conversation and in the dialogue 'reality is crystalised, narrowed and stabilised. Ambivalences are converted to certainties. Typifications of self and others become more settled' (p. 316). In their model social reality is constructed in and through marriage, a relationship that is the epitome of the personal and the private. Their analysis emphasises creative intimacy, where conversations are unscripted and partners are social strangers to one another, and not social obligation. It denies the inequalities of domestic power which shape 'the conversation' and the impact of familistic policies. However, their analysis has made its own ironic contribution to family ideology as their arguments have been extensively reprinted in journals of family therapists and advisers, adding impetus to the popular spread of companionate expectations of marriage.

Modern marriage stresses companionship and the importance of the couple. A good marriage is seen as a relationship founded on love, invested with personal commitment and looked to for mutual support and satisfaction. Discussions of companionacy are often falsely juxtaposed to those of patriarchy, but the emphasis on mutuality contributes to the strength of patriarchy not its diminution. Companionship in marriage should not be confused with equality in marriage and its importance does not rest with its factuality. What is important is not the existence/non-existence of conjugal mutuality but the ideology of domestic partnership. Past discussions have frequently failed to distinguish these aspects of analysis and, as Harris argues, failed 'to keep distinct the concepts in which informants describe their relationships and the analytic concepts of the sociological observer' (1983, p. 227). People use the language of mutuality to describe their commitment to the relationship, but the commitment to marriage is distinct from the divisions and inequalities of being married. In the language of marriage, jointness is not the same as symmetry, and partnership does not necessitate equality.

Companionacy is linked to patriarchy in Western definitions of conjugality. The cultural ethos of Western society gives priority to the relationship between husband and wife. As Greer argues, 'the relationship takes precedence over all others, and involves more time and more attentions than are given to any other blood relationship . . . even the children of the nuclear unit' (1985, p. 222). For Greer, women in contemporary Western marriage are required to be unfailingly available to their husbands for sexual pleasure and for domestic labour. Here the home is a domestic play area for men, the castle of their personal autonomy where each husband has 'unlimited power to brutalise his wife as well as to please her' (ibid, p. 251).

Companionacy also links through conjugality to the privacy of the home and marital relationships. With industrialisation and the separation of home and work, women were redefined as specialist homemakers and men as specialist workers in the newly emerged sexual division of labour. Around this division the bourgeoisie constructed a romantic vision of home and family life, a refuge from the harsh outside world, a haven for domestic virtue and female sensibility and a proper place for women. The bourgeoisie of the last century articulated an ideological divide between public and private spheres of existence, between home and the world of politics and commerce. Women and womanly virtue were identified with this private sphere and wifehood became synonymous with housecraft, motherhood and domesticity (Davidoff and Hall, 1987). As a private place the home was seen as an area of choice, of secrecy, of activities set apart from state interference and the world of work. Central to what was 'private' were relationships between husband and wife and hence the rules of domestic privacy licensed men to wield the power of the purse and the power of the fist unchallenged within the home. In marriage the privatisation of women serves to individualise their circumstances and to maintain their continued dependence on men. Outside conventional marriage the living arrangements of women are subject to more scrutiny by state agencies and by neighbours. The privacy of the home appears to be more the privacy of men, and women do not have the same entitlement to be respected in their domestic castles.

The model of companionate marriage relates to class. Partnership in marriage is a bourgeois construct whose hegemony may influence the working class or ethnic minorities, but never emanates from them. When it does touch them, it does so only peripherally. In blue-collar marriage bread-and-butter survival in a grim economic climate is a central concern and companionacy appears a luxury for the better-off. If modern marriage can be viewed as a dialogue, Rubin (1976) and Komarovsky (1962) offer classic analyses of marital silence. Their accounts of the emotional barrennes of working-class marriage is a measure of their own assumptions about married life. It has been among middle-class couples that companionacy in marriage has been most self-consciously approached (Edgell, 1980). Here the sense of sharing was crucial even if the division of domestic power fell short of what could be considered egalitarian. A similar logic can be applied to women without husbands, where cohabitation may acquire differential class logics and the reactions to loss and dissolution link to class constructions of domestic relationships.

Mutuality in marriage has an uneven connection with gender, bringing greater commitment from women to the relationship. Companionacy has a firmer association with women and wives than men and husbands and analyses of marital happiness note the premium that women place on friendship and emotional satisfaction in marriage. Mansfield and Collard in their interviews with young newly-weds found that men and women have different expectations of intimacy and different interpretations of togetherness. 'Most (though not all) men seek a *life in common* with their wives, a home life, a physical and psychological base; somewhere and someone to set out from and to. But for nearly all wives, their desired marriage was *a common life* with an empathetic partner, who would provide both material and emotional security' (1988, p. 179).

This implies the greater reliance of contemporary women on male partners and problematises the lives of women without partners as much as those with. It raises questions of emotional and social support and of how women construct a family life not built around the couple. The assumptions of coupledom may make life outside marriage more intolerable or the model of conjugal togetherness may be rejected as women define themselves in other ways. Perhaps the search for mutuality is an overrated goal, since what it brings to marriage is dreariness and boredom. More detachment between men and women may then bring more autonomy and more sexual fun, where relationships have a freshness and unpredictability, free from the tedium of a continuous marital conversation. For other women, while the ties of marriage may be increasingly irrelevant, the pursuit of companionship within 'a relationship' may be as strong as ever.

Sexuality

Companionacy is about friendship in marriage, a theme that may sit uncomfortably with sexuality. Women are expected to be more companionable than men, since mutuality fits more readily with the feminine attribute of nurturance, and the image of the caring/sharing husband is an emasculated one. Bernard (1972) argues that the structure of sexuality in Western society is at odds with companionship; one cannot befriend a lover. Oakley (1984) arrives at a similar conclusion, finding her personal dilemma illustrative of the more general war between love and the family. Here men want 'the conveniences of marriage and the freedom of the sexual chase. [And] . . . women want sexual joy and security to be combined in the same person: their image of men is an integrated one. Therefore the desires of men and women are incompatible . . . because women can't find in men whole human beings, and the whole human beings women are, are not the women men have been led to believe they want' (p. 121).

Monogamous marriage presumes sexual possession and patriarchy ensures that sexual possession is traditionally more the prerogative of husbands than wives. There have been greater claims for equality in sexuality, especially since the 1960s. This was thought a time of sexual revolution and liberation, with the availability of contraception and the atmosphere of permissiveness. Pre-marital sexual experience has increased since the 1960s for women, and Lawson (1989) claims that adultery is practised as much by young wives as young husbands, but women remain on average less sexually experienced when first marrying than men. Mansfield and Collard's survey found that, although pre-nuptial virginity is now rare, 'Among the brides, just over half had had a sexual relationship with someone else as well as their spouse, whereas amongst two-thirds of husbands had done so' (1988, p. 179). Fidelity is an essential ingredient of most marriages and adultery is the main grounds for divorce cited by male petitioners.

The domestic expression of sexuality is mediated both by assumptions of marriage and by the power of men. Coveney and her colleagues (1984) argue that a male definition of sexuality divides women into the pure and the fallen and blames their sexual use and abuse on the nature of the women themselves. Male sexuality is given a biological grounding in theories of sexuality which attribute men with a natural and irresistible need for outlet and gratification. The sexual revolution has made little difference, merely increasing male assumptions about the availability of women outside marriage and incorporating domestic sexuality into companionate models of marriage for women inside marriage. In the latter case sex therapy and sex manuals are available to those who feel that mutual sexual pleasure falls short of the ideal. The sex in sexology is utilitarian, not passionate, and men are encouraged to engage in considerate coitus. Sexology furthers the compliance of women to male sexuality, often normalising what was regarded as perversity, in a regime where 'anything goes' between what are seen as equal and consenting partners. Sexology appears to promote a genderless 'unisexuality' but is bound by wider patterns of power and consent in marriage and it is still often an adjunct to masculinist definitions of the sexual chase.

What consequences does this then have for the sexuality of women in their detachment from marriage? On a personal level it may bring greater freedom or greater availability to men, or it may usher in the temporary or permanent end of women's sex lives. This issue is mediated by age and ageism, seen as irrelevant for the elderly widow, but a critical issue for the young divorcee. Also the issue of sexual identity for women without husbands influences a wide spectrum of relationships, tinging friendship patterns with both men and women.

Marriage and female biography

The normality of marriage is evidenced by its prominent part in life-cycle models of the individual and the family. Marriage is seen as a normal stage of human development and as the entrée into a new family life. Individuals are born, mature and die and families are formed, change and dissolve. These changes of the individual and families have been summarised in cyclical models, where stages are built around what are considered the main tasks of family life, of getting married, having children, of bringing those children up and launching them into the wider community. Marriage is fitted into a natural history of humanity, with a vocabulary based on the avian metaphor of nest-building: newly married and older couples occupy 'unused' and 'empty nests', from which fledgling children have flown or been launched. Recently the new category of the 'crowded nest' has been coined to summarise the domestic pressures of youth unemployment and housing shortage. It also has a semi-mystical connotation, placing biography within an unending stream of life.

The life-cycle model makes assumptions about typical individuals and typical families and offers a conventional and family-centred view of biography, especially female biography, where it tends to link the main developmental tasks of women to hearth and home. It connotes normality and inevitability, assuming that all women will marry, will desire and if possible have children inside marriage, will not become separated, divorced or remarried, and will not become widows until their children have grown up and left home. The model ties women to marriage and to childbirth. It offers a traditional statement on women where the combined pathway of marriage and motherhood is the route for all women.

In recent years the family life-cycle model has attracted criticism for its insensitivity to biographical differences and for containing an implicit prescription for women's lives. For some the model is seen as less useful because of changing family forms. Allan argues that, 'Whereas a generation ago it was quite sensible to analyse domestic circumstances in terms of the "family life cycle" – implying a more or less structured set of stages through which families passed from marriage to death – it is far less so now' (1985, p. 2). Murphy (1983) has estimated that less than half of British women currently in their twenties will pass through the stages of child-rearing and long-term marriage and the figure is even lower in the USA. However, to claim that the model was applicable in the past, and no longer applicable today, overestimates the stability and permanence of historic marriages and misses its ideological import.

The model also contains another confusion. Its arguments attempt to encompass distinct levels of analysis as it moves between biographical stages in an individual's life and household units in family change. Families do not have lives and an individual's life-span is not a cycle. The family life-cycle is a phrase fraught with ambiguity and an attempt to submerge women, their life experiences and identities in aggregate forms and to see their life interests as coterminous with the family. In the family life-cycle the variability of women's experiences becomes largely invisible.

To resolve some of these issues, more recent sociological analysis has used the model of the life-course (Elder, 1978; Hareven, 1982; Cohen, 1987). 'The life course refers to the pathways through the age-differentiated life span, to social patterns in timing, duration, spacing and order of events' (Elder, 1978) and, in this model, women's lives appear more dynamic and diverse. The new emphasis is on plurality of pathways, variable timings of transitions and 'more flexible biographical patterns within a continually changing social system' (Cohen, 1987, p. 1). Using the perspective of the life-course it is possible to draw out differing threads of individual lives and examine the ways in which these threads combine. Hence marriage careers can be set against patterns of family building and participation in paid employment without these elements forming a single prescriptive whole. Life-course information is also more easily grounded in the narrative of life-history accounts. As such, the categories which derive from its use seem more emergent and less imposed on biographical data, as well as more sensitive to gender and the variation in the domestic, marital and familial relationships of women.

Life-course analysis also captures contemporary feeling and is evocative of greater uncertainty and insecurity as well as flexibility in people's lives. While the model has analytic advantages, it also has a number of weaknesses. It portrays women as the mistresses of their own fate and it individualises their circumstances. As invididuals age within an historical context, the pathways of their lives appear idiosyncratic and the extent to which they are navigating their own journeys is often exaggerated. The life-course model is apolitical and voluntaristic, ignoring the wider ways in which the lives of women are shaped by 'the family' and their options structured by the normality of marriage and children. Marriage is more than a probable stage in an individual's life-course, but a grounding to normal family life.

Marriage is an important transition point for young women as they move towards adulthood. Securing a job or embarking on a career is the major transition for a man, but for women this is overshadowed by marriage. The desire to marry is more prominent in young women's ambitions, and in Mansfield and Collard's study (1988) more women were identified as marriage-seekers. Marriage makes domesticity a major new area of interest for women, the entry into which is celebrated with the social pomp of the 'proper wedding'. In male biography marriage focuses men's interest beyond the home, committing them to breadwinning. Hence it is not coincidental that there is no magazine called 'Bridegroom'.

Marriage, in making women's transition to adulthood, is closely associated with a home of their own and modern marriage is postponed until couples can form an independent household. Macfarlane (1978) has linked the independence of the marital household to the spirit of individualism and he claims that this, in Britain, long pre-dated industrialism and modernity. The absence of marriage, however, did not preclude the development of a sexual relationship or the birth of children. Similar attitudes are found today and Wallace describes how young women may postpone marriage, but not necessarily cohabitation or motherhood, until they can have 'a real wedding and the accoutrements of a real home' (1987, p. 120). Marriage forms women into homemakers, a process mediated by class, where a husband in regular work is a more marriageable proposition.

Another aspect of this debate is the heritage of marriage in the lives of women who are no longer married. Exiting from marriage does not remove all ties of marriage. Delphy (1984) regarded divorce as marriage in another form and the continuation of co-parenting makes this especially so. The circumstances of widows reflect the provision made for them by their husbands. The heritage of former marriages may follow women into new relationships and second and subsequent marriage partnerships may differ from earlier ones.

Marriage is not merely a particular route or a stopping-off point for women since the domestic options are not equally valued by the individual or valorised in social structure. The variability of marriage and family relationships continues to be subsumed within the normality of marriage. Marriage remains prominent in many young women's ambitions, as the basis of personal happiness and female fulfilment. It is seen as the outcome of romance, the site of love and accepted place for women to express their sexuality. The imagery of marriage is that of partnership, mutual support and of individual personalities merged into the corporate identities of couples. This image remains despite the gross and subtle variations in women's life-time connection to marriage.

Analytic problems

So far, comparing and contrasting the circumstances of women with husbands to women without husbands has been advanced as a more or less straightforward task. But there are some difficulties. The differences between these groups of women may be socially unclear and the ideological strength of marriage generates problems of comparison.

First, distinguishing the cohabiting from the married is difficult, as is the argument that cohabitation is an alternative to marriage. There are conceptual problems and fieldwork difficulties when non-marital terminology is sought for other forms of heterosexual and residential partnership. All are awkward and unsatisfactory. 'Cohabitee' appears too formal, 'partner' appears too business-like or uncommitted, 'girl/boyfriend' appears too juvenile and 'lover' too sexual. Frequently these alternatives are incorporated within a general frame of marriage, or derive their meaning from it. State statistics on household composition and marital status direct a cohabitee to be reclassified as *de facto* spouse. Here cohabitation has an ambiguous status. Although the state assumes men are supporting women with whom they cohabit, it is a moot point whether cohabitation does or should have the legal equivalence of marriage. These definitional problems grow in cross-cultural comparison, where attempts at a universal definition of marriage are so often the mask for ethnocentricity.

However, extending the terminology of marriage to include various states of heterosexual 'living together' precludes popular or theoretical consideration of alternatives. Also the assumption that, whatever their legal status, co-residential and heterosexual relationships equate with marriage, with all its ramifications, may do violence to people's intentions, since they may not marry because they do not want a married relationship. Béjin (1985) notes the prevalance of living together among the young and regards this 'juvenile cohabitation' as an attempt to bridge the great divide between bread-and-butter love in marriage and passionate love outside. It is an attempt to secure the best of both worlds with its more negotiated commitments, its emotional importance and its partial acceptance in society. Although young people may wish to establish a new type of relationship, the hegemony of marriage is intrinsic to its institutional strength and it is a framework for the normalisation of domestic relationships.

Second, other complications arise in discussion of the supposed population of lone parents. Here there are single women who are not alone and married women whose husbands are periodically or permanently away. Here are found the key examples of families that do not live together and 'families' who live together without kinship tie. This has clear implications for the economic and social support. In the codification of family obligations Finch notes two different principles in establishing liability. 'They are: the principle of genealogical relationship; the principle of mutual support between adults who share a household' (1989, p. 121). In the disjunction between kinship relations and household membership, the support of women without husbands provides the wide scope for policy ambiguity and personal wrangling.

Third, the very ideology of the family presents obstacles to the answering of these questions since it encourages the outward 'normalisation' of atypical family forms. Cornwell (1984) commented on the ways in which discrepant information on aspects of marital relationships were fitted into the conventional frame via 'public moralities'. Similarly Burgoyne notes, in her analysis of step-families, how 'factual responses . . . were somewhat eclipsed by their desire to portray their present partnership and the family unit they had created as an improvement on what had gone before' (1986, p. 9). While these respondents tried to normalise their relationships, purveyors of public morality may attempt to do the opposite. Women without husbands have a poor public image, being seen as sad or inadequate, as economic leeches or strident individualists, as rejected or redundant. Here the primacy given to conventional family relationships means that the differences in relationships between these and atypical families are exaggerated and linked to other social problems.

There are, then, diverse points of comparison that relate to the status of marriage and non-marriage and the nature of relationships in quasi- and partial marriage. There are arguments about the extent to which cohabitation and even divorce are forms of marriage. In husband-absence there are the issues of how far women act as *de facto* lone wives and the impact of this on their marriages. There are also issues of how far current circumstance connects to biographical context. Among single women the circumstances of the never-married are distinct from those of the once-married and an historic heritage of marriage in women's lives is a vital factor.

Conclusion

Today many women live outside matrimony, with the rise in divorce and cohabitation and the large numbers of elderly widows. On the level of relationships there are also women who, for occupational and custodial reasons, do not regularly live with their husbands. These relationships suggest some fragmentation of the traditional model of women, where mother is not linked with wife and neither presumes co-residence. These trends are also coincident with the continued importance of marriage and the vibrant political defence of the family. To discuss the circumstances of the disparate group of women who constitute women without husbands is not to discuss issues that are different or distinct from marriage and 'the family', but merely an examination of marriage from a different vantage point.

Patriarchy influences the lives of all women and the lack or absence of a husband may give women more immediate control of the household but without escaping from any of the wider patriarchal structures. Without a male breadwinner, they may be more economically vulnerable and real self-sufficiency may continue to elude them in a sexually divided labour market. Patriarchy adds ambivalence to their dealings with the state, since they are the main recipients of welfare in a system which tries to encourage two-parent families. Here state policies are caught in a dilemma in seeking to give no financial advantage to single parenthood while simultaneously trying to prevent child poverty. Economically and politically the defence of the family appears to rest on the misery of those outside it.

Marriage is a strong determinant of the personal and social lives of women. Women without husbands must look elsewhere for companionship, support and sexual pleasure. Here they may find more freedom, but it is in a world of couples, where the rules of conjugality mean that 'relationships outside marriages have become thinner and less meaningful' (Barrett and McIntosh, 1982). Conventional marriage also structures the domestic relations, powers and routines of women around a husband and it remains an empirical question the extent to which these are reformulated in a husband's absence. Similarly, in the household, the triadic relationship between two resident parents and children becomes dyadic when there is only one parent. With the dissolution of marriage 'the family' is dispersed between households where a wider range of adults have a parental or quasi-parental interest in the children, or children may even lose contact altogether with the absent parent now with a new partner. All this changes the shape of the interactive knots that are the sub-text of normal family life and sets the agenda for women without husbands. They also form the themes for discussion in subsequent chapters.

4

Emotional and personal lives

Many women without husbands were once conventionally married or in stable partnerships. When women find themselves on their own there is change and frequently trauma, new circumstances to deal with and new identities to forge. In these new circumstances, as with the discussion on the degrees of marriage, there are degrees of husband absence. In a psychological, as well as a physical sense, husbands are more or less present in the lives of lone women. Women's adjustment involves processes of personal change, the construction of new ways of behaving and the creation of new avenues for the expression of companionship and sexuality. This chapter is about the emotional processes of becoming single and/or alone, the social psychology and the emotional survival of women at the margins and beyond marriage.

The growing stress on the psychology of marital relationships has been mirrored in preoccupation with personal loss and psychic adjustment when marriages dissolve and couples are separated. This sometimes makes it hard to describe the structural features of marital dissolution in the West because the area is so redolent with emotion, but nonetheless these emotions, while not forming the complete picture, deserve some attention.

The dissolution of marriage and husband absence

The marriages of women become attenuated in a number of ways and there are similarities and differences between them. Bereavement, divorce and residential separation have in different ways and to different degrees been seen as emotionally trying for women. All are sad and unpleasant circumstances to be coped with and all unleash negative feelings, which women have in some way to resolve.

Bereavement

Bereavement is seen as amongst the most traumatic of human experiences which stirs a gamut of emotions and feelings that border on those of the physically ill and the mentally disturbed. Parkes (1986) offers a vivid picture of adult grief. The death of a partner renders the world a different place to live in and the widow has many changes of identity and circumstance to which to become accustomed. Normal grief is a difficult and prolonged process, where there is both flight and fight. The bereaved often begin by denying loss and bottling feelings to gain more time for adjustment, and to prevent grief from overwhelming the psyche. This co-exists with weeping, howling and the confrontation of pain. The initial loss is frequently accompanied by physical feelings of numbness and unreality. When this gives way, it is to acute pangs of yearning for the dead person. As these diminish, through pining to nostalgia, there is the danger of a more continuous and steady state of depression, especially as the other changes of domestic routine – household responsibility, social life and economic circumstances – also present themselves.

Bereavement brings pyschic pain and this appears to be a necessary part of 'grief work', where it is not that the anguish is smoothed away as memories fade, but confronted in the repetition of poignant memories. The past is trawled and retrawled for the sad facts to be fully known, appreciated and reorganised to make fresh sense of changed lives and human tragedy. This is what is meant by coming to terms with widowhood. Within the grief work, marital history is rewritten as husbands are idealised and marriages are remembered as happier than they were, and from the grief work a new identity emerges as well as fresh problems. For women who have spent many years learning to live with their husbands, to learn to live without them is a difficult and frustrating process. This is especially so where the man has been the manifestly dominant partner, in a marriage which encased the woman in dependence and diminished her capacity to function on her own. It is also more difficult where the husband has been ill for some time before death and the wife has undertaken the demanding roles of informal carer and nurse. Because of the intensity of commitment, and despite the exhaustion, there is often little relief in death, as in these circumstances it brings a bigger emptiness.

Grief erodes feelings of good health and makes women more susceptible to illness. It can also spill over into mental illness. Here Parkes refers to abnormal grieving and this occurs when the woman fails to complete the grief work and where she is too swamped by guilt and self-reproach to recover and let go of the dead person. Anger is a common aspect of grief, and if it is directed at doctors and God it is not so destructive for relationships as if it is directed at family members and friends, and if it does not diminish. Social isolation increases with widowhood, but 'abnormal grieving' makes this worse. However, the difference between normal and abnormal grief is one of intensity and prolongation not of nature. Intense grieving is also not a sign of a good marriage as there are some indications that women more dissatisfied with their marriages find it harder to recover from the death of their husbands.

Whatever the depth of the grief there are factors that help it to be eased. Traditional funeral and mortuary rites help in the acceptance of death and give ritual expression to bereavement although Gorer's proposition that English culture encourages a denial of mourning (1965) has not been seriously challenged. The hospice movement plays an increasingly important part today in the preparation of individuals and their families for death. Death has no acceptable place in hospitals geared to a curative frame, and at time to relentless treatment, since here it is a sign of failure. Hospices are about acceptance and inevitability and give women a good start for their grief work. And after the death of their husbands there are pressure groups and self-help organisations which counsel widows and lobby on their behalf.

Contemporary social psychology has sought to normalise grief, by distinguishing its normal from its pathological forms and by seeing it as a development task for the individual and an area of appropriate intervention by therapists and counsellors (Schuchter, 1986). Such an approach emphasises the meaning of grief for the individual. By contrast Prior (1989) is concerned with the social patterning of grief. He examined the numbers and the types of citations for dead persons that were placed in Belfast newspapers and found some striking differences. Among the Belfast middle class, obituary notices were fewer in number and informative in nature which implies that for the middle class mourning is a more private, family-based affair. When the deceased had been married citations were more numerous. Prior argues that this reflects the greater disruption that death brings to the living and in particular the greater dislocation that death brings to the lives of widows and widowers.

Divorce

Emotional reactions to divorce are frequently compared to those in bereavement and although both involve trauma and learning to become unmarried, there are differences. The emotional structure of divorce contains more ambivalence. Divorce is rarely a mutual decision and Kaslow and Schwartz (1987) suggest that only in 15 per cent of cases do couples jointly decide on this course of action. The individual's emotions are influenced by their role in the initiation of proceedings and these include those bereft at having been rejected and those relieved at ending a failed marriage. But whoever initiates the process there is little enjoyment in it for anyone and all those involved describe it as harrowing. At best divorce is a relief and relationships are civilised and cordial. Feeling rejected and angry that the person has left you is common in mourning, but for the divorcee the feeling is often based in fact and not in metaphor. Furthermore, divorcees are already emotionally estranged, since it is the resolution of this that is the whole purpose of the divorce. Emotional detachment is intrinsic to the process of divorce itself, not a sad but inevitable by-product of loss, as in death. Finally, the public image of the divorcee is also more ambivalent. The divorced woman attracts less sympathy than the widow, and divorce, unlike death by natural causes, is seen as somebody's fault. Divorcees feel they have failed to make a go of things and are gripped both by guilt and the desire to blame the other person.

The books that offer advice to those divorcing often describe the experience as an 'inner journey', the processes of uncoupling and of learning to be single again. There are close analogies between this and 'grief work', but 'divorce work' is less clearly defined and harder to complete. There are no rituals that mark the change, although orthodox Judaism is something of an exception, as here there is religious pronouncement and some ceremony in the granting of divorce. Also, whatever the commitment to a clean break, divorce does not have the finality of death and, especially where there are children, women have ex-husbands rather than no husbands at all. Finally, the continuation of some sort of contact with an ex-husband, and the influence of this on relations with children and wider kin, inevitably brings a political dimension to the situation. If you view divorce as something to be individually worked out, it can be seen as the continuation of the marital conversation. This working-out may involve contest and revenge in relations and the use of children as weapons. In divorce, there continue to be tugs of loyalty and permutations of allegiance which are impossible following bereavement.

The experience of divorce also varies with the circumstances of the woman. Those who have been married longer and have no outside employment find divorce a more devastating experience. Unsurprisingly, those who have built their lives more completely around marriage are more bereft when that marriage dissolves. Again, as with bereavement, divorce undermines feelings of well-being and women are more likely to experience health problems and consult their doctor while it is on-going and in its aftermath.

Husband absence

Life without the daily presence of a husband is of a different order from bereavement and divorce, but it is a circumstance unanimously regarded in the literature as stressful. It has been empirically associated with depression and anxiety and disrupted patterns of eating and sleeping. The measurement of stress levels for lone wives has also been accompanied by assessment of their coping strategies and their efficacy as lone wives. The classic account of the problems of husband absence is found in Isay's formulation of the Submariners' Wives Syndrome (1968). He found rage and depression, where wives react with neurosis and retaliate with infidelity while husbands are away and frigidity when they come home. Although based on a clinical population of wives who attended a psychiatric clinic attached to a submarine base Isay generalised his findings to typify common reactions to occupational separation from husbands. The wives presenting problems were the pathological tip of an iceberg of widespread stress. As with grief and divorce, discussions of husband absence raise questions on pathological and normal behaviour for women.

However, Isay goes further and comments on their social behaviour: wives 'regress' by rekindling links with their parents and sometimes returning to them; they assume the 'traditionally masculine responsibilities' of household management and resent their surrender when husbands return. Rules of coupledom are hard to apply when husbands are not there, but greater independence for lone wives often provokes anxiety in the marriage. There are tacit divisions between wives who do and do not cope but it is often unclear what constitutes adequate coping. There is the suggestion that wives who cope too well, both psychologically and in the management of their homes, are more likely to exit from their marriages and the conclusion that the stability of their marriage assumes some personal distress and practical difficulties when husbands are away. Where there is little anger or impairment, this is taken as evidence of wives bottling their feelings or of their uncaringness and lack of commitment to their husbands and their marriages.

Similar 'syndromes' have been found elsewhere. A Scottish study of women married to off-shore oil workers (Morrice, 1981; Morrice *et al.*, 1985; Taylor *et al.*, 1985) also found 'anxiety, depression and sexual difficulties' in clinical observations of this group and this was backed by the assumptions of local doctors and social workers. A research programme was mounted to gauge the levels of 'psycho-social morbidity', with a view to establishing a preventative counselling service. For Isay (1968) the anxiety of women peaked just prior to a husband's return, while in the Scottish study (Taylor *et al.*, 1985) it was high only when men were away working off-shore. Furthermore, the hypotheses of the research were not entirely confirmed. When the reported levels of anxiety or depression among oil wives and their assessment of their own health or their consultation rates with doctors were compared with national levels, little difference was found.

However the question remains as to why these women were seen as a problem group by professionals in the community and why false comparisons were drawn between these women and others co-resident with their husbands. The research also sought to measure behavioural change and marital conflict. Here it concluded that wives recently married and experiencing irregular husband absence had the most adverse behavioural and emotional reactions and it was women in paid employment who experienced the most marital conflict. These findings raise a number of points. It is not just absence, but the rhythms of coming and going which are important, and women's attitude towards husband absence relates to their other identities and their experience of marriage itself.

Case-study material on naval wives (Chandler, 1987) describes both a range of reactions to a husband's absence and return, and the complexity of emotions. Women who recounted the black despair of a husband's departure also described the peace of time to themselves while he was away. There was the loneliness of his absence and the disruption of his return. There was the longing for the homecoming and the anticlimax of reunion. Challenge and excitement are the other side of insecurity and loneliness and the unpredictability of husband absence could add drama to humdrum marriage. Marriages punctuated by separation may be more painful, but they are also more romantic. Husband absence provoked in women a roller-coaster of emotion. They prepared by increasing emotional distance which gave way to mood swings prior to departure. They fought a sense of desertion, constructed a new way of life in his absence and were gripped by a certain apprehension on his return. Women recalled instances of panic, of blowing small problems out of proportion and intermittent bouts of desolation. Many gave personal testimony of how they had learned to make the best of their husbands being away and even to enjoy this form of marriage. It was not a matter of them coping or not coping. They all coped. But many did not enjoy the situations they coped with and felt that they should not have to manage these situations alone. Throughout, the dominant attitude was one where they gritted their teeth and got on with life and their comments were full of a sense of injustice, not incapacity. As conventional marriage increasingly stresses the mutuality of couples, lone wives are less able to find a rationale for their circumstance.

There is also some doubt about which is more problematic, the absence of the husband or his return and reintegration within the home. In many occupations spells away are matched by equally long spells at home and here Solheim's study or Norwegian oil workers (1984) is enlightening. It is also a rare study in that it focuses as much on men's reactions to absence and return as on women's. These oil workers had originally been attracted to the job by the opportunities it gave them to spend time with their wives and children, where every three weeks spent on the rig was matched by a fortnight at home. Yet ironically those most committed to shared family activities found both the time at home and the extensive time away unsatisfactory, as did their wives, and this was especially so if the wife was in paid employment outside the home. After a time the men's enthusuasm for DIY jobs palled, and if they saw their leave times as holiday-like, they preferred their wives to be at home with them. But wives resented these pressures for intermittent but intense togetherness as much as their isolation when men went back to the rigs. Long leaves frequently turned into an unstructured and debilitating time at home with families, fraught with marital conflict, and this conflict was greater among those committed to a more companionate approach to marriage, with its stress on mutuality.

Women in husband-absent marriages have a social identity more closely connected with conventional married relationships. Unlike the divorced and the bereaved, they are less able and not expected to forge new identities for themselves, since theirs is not an adjustment to loss or dissolution and they remain married even though their husbands are not there. The anxieties of women again connect with a bourgeois view of conjugality, where the onus of adaptability is placed firmly on the wife. This contrasts with Tunstall's account of working-class life and the marriages of trawlermen (1962). This study reflects a different era of research and wives are described largely without reference to their anxiety or their personal adjustment. These women were conscious of the material benefits they derived from the relatively high earning of their husbands, were pleased to see them return from fishing trips and after a few days even more pleased to see them return to sea. These women lived in the context of close kin and home town and their dependence on men was described as primarily economic not emotional, although Tunstall did describe some common difficulties in their marriages. While not emphasising the psychology of the situation, he noted the ambivalence in the attitudes of both husbands and wives: wives looked forward to the visits of their husbands so long as they did not overstay their welcome; husbands thought that wives should be self-reliant and good managers but, if they were too good at managing and too self-reliant, men felt loved only for their pay-packets and not for themselves.

The social psychology of loss, dissolution and absence

There are common themes in the reactions of women to loss and absence. For all, being without a husband creates a gap in their daily lives, but there are also other problems to contend with. There are new household routines and responsibilities and a new context in which to interact with others. Morgan (1985) talks about the importance of personal projects and planning in family life and these are abruptly broken, or harder to sustain, when husbands are missing. There are the difficulties of forging a new identity and of making sense of a world which disparages women who are alone. Also there is the cost of commitment to marriage as women who invest more in their marriage may find functioning without a husband proportionately more difficult.

Loss traumatises women, absence makes them anxious and both make them psychosomatically ill. A sense of health and well-being connect with a positive view of oneself and this is hard to sustain in a social system where women without husbands are marginalised. Also social support is an ingredient of good health (Blaxter, 1989). While analyses of women without husbands need to be sensitive to the social construction of anxiety and the language of stress, lethargy and illness, they must ensure that reactions to dissolution and absence are not falsely contrasted with the happiness of normal family life. Guilt, manipulation and scapegoating thrive in normal families and 'the allocation of blame is part of the regular small change of family living' (Morgan, 1985, p. 141). The exhibition and recounting of suffering is not a simple quasi-biological reaction but part of the drama and politics of the home. The lack of a husband can also be used by women as a peg on which to hang all the shortcomings of their lives, where everything would be better were they to live as part of a conventional couple.

Apart from expressed emotion, patterns of eating and sleeping are common indices of distress among women, but these too are not wholly biological events – they are also social. It would be odd if the absence of a significant member of the household did not alter these behaviours, though alteration is not the same as disturbance. If the production of nourishing and filling meals and eating them with your husband is part of being a wife, his absence may alter the whole *pattern* of eating and this goes beyond the issue of women eating straightforwardly more or less. Murcott notes the centrality of cooking to housecraft and the obligation of wives to produce 'proper meals' for household members. 'If husbands and children are absent, women alone will not "cook", indeed, may not even eat. It is the others' presence which provides the rationale for women turning to and making a proper meal' (1983, p. 85). Within the description of lone women 'not eating' there is no recognition of the freedom of serial meals, 'grazing' in the fridge and just living on snacks. Similarly Western culture assumes that husband and wife sleep together and his absence from the bed may create strangeness rather than stress.

The chapter has dealt with emotional problems, but it could be argued that many of the problems faced by women without husbands would be misclassified if they were identified only as emotional problems, although emotions do attach to them. For instance, boredom and loneliness are commonly reported by women without husbands, but to regard these as emotional problems implies that they exist primarily in the minds and attitudes of women. Women report that they are lonely because they are socially isolated and marginalised in society built around couples and the conventionally married.

In responding to loss, dissolution and absence there are significant variations. There are differences in the extent to which the women are able to develop a new identity. Life without a husband demands more personal responsibility from women and gives them more power. The emotional and economic survival of women without husbands is incompatible with a doll's-house mentality. Here women whose partners are only temporarily absent are in the most anomalous position. They are not traumatised by loss, the absence is only temporary, as a group they are less socially visible and they are not seen as having the same entitlement to emotional or practical difficulties. There is also the strange problem of women who appear to cope too well. When husbands are away, although they are *de facto* lone wives, they are expected to behave as married women and keep their husband's place open for him when he returns. Loss is diminished but ambiguity is magnified and this is especially so where marriage adopts a bourgeois form and the assumptions of close-knit mutuality. Women temporarily without husbands are acutely aware of their awkward social situation, where they are married but have no husband, and often feel uncomfortable with both their married and their single friends.

A strong theme in the area is the relationship between disengagement from marriage and mental illness in women but, whatever the speculation, there is little systematic comparison of neurosis among women conventionally married and women without husbands. Although there have been long-standing analyses of the personal costs incurred by women in marriage, conventional family life is seen paradoxically as the basis of mental health, not as generating psychic disorder. Laing and Esterson (1970) described the psychological jungle that forms the intimate world of the family, but these ideas no longer have the popularity that they enjoyed over a decade ago. Durkheim (1952) demonstrated that marriage inhibited suicide among men, but for married women there was a substantially lower 'coefficient of preservation'. Bernard (1973) concluded that marriage was not good for women and contrasted their poorer mental and emotional health with that of men and with that of women who had remained single and by implication independent.

More recent and broadly-based surveys confirm their arguments. Brown and Harris (1978) found that two-thirds of all married women with a pre-school child suffered fully or marginally from clinical depression, as did 17 per cent of all women in their study. Miles (1988) describes the greater preponderance of neurotic and depressive disorders amongst women, especially those who are married. Such findings have been integrated into a feminist critique of marriage and analyses of its destructive impact on women, but the issue is complex once you attempt to explain their increased propensity for poor mental health. The social circumstances of married women, the alienating influences of housework and the balancing of pressures from home and work, have been identified as more stressful than those of men. Emotional instability can be seen as a component of female personality and Oakley (1982) has argued that it is a main ingredient in the construction of womanhood and feminity, where neurosis is an exaggeration of their sensitivity and an augmentation of their 'expressive orientation'. Also the medicalisation of women's problems individualises their difficulties and depoliticises their circumstances.

Miles (1988) sees the greater identification of women as mentally ill as consequent on their lack of power in wider society and its dismissive sex stereotyping. 'Neurotic' has a double meaning and implies that such women are troublesome and lacking in self-control, as much as being 'ill'. Finally Busfield (1983) adds another dimension to the debate. The arguments that mental disorder results from gender typing in the emotionality and irrationality of women or is a consequence of the greater stressfulness of women's lives are both problematic. Neither argument is wholly supportable since the very construction of mental disorder is not gender free and 'the psychiatric conceptualisations of different mental illness are fashioned and created in ways that are often gender specific' (p. 131).

A final aspect of the psychology of women without husbands, and one of the commonest occurrences in grief, is the continued sense of the presence of a husband. He is often felt to be near, is glimpsed in the street and appears in vivid dreams. He may be closely associated with particular objects, and in a metaphysical sense the living always continue to carry the dead within them. Western society is unusual in its dismissal of spirits as other cultures more readily acknowledge animism and recognise the presence of dead ancestors in people's daily lives. Women may symbolically maintain a husband's presence in the home with pictures and objects and they may mentally refer to his imagined wishes when making decisions. This means that in the world of domestic meaning some husbands may be more absent from home than others and their place in the domestic symbol system may be poorly correlated with their physical presence.

The new identity

Part of the personal change encompassed in bereavement, dissolution and absence is the construction of a new identity for women. Being on their own increases their independence, their self-sufficiency and their choice, but the down-side of these new feelings is loneliness and insecurity. Again it is important not to exaggerate differences, as studies of conventional marriage show that loneliness and material insecurity can flourish in officially intact relationships, although they may be felt more acutely when women are on their own. There is also the issue of sexual frustration. For those in husband-absent marriages, the options for resolution are narrower, where, for those who wish to remain married, it is seen as safer to accept being alone. Women view their new situation in a variety of ways. There are those who eventually become resigned to changed circumstances, others who set about creating an independent life-style with gusto and there are those who seek a new relationship.

Establishing new relationships with men is not easy, as the social world divides into a hemisphere of couples, where lone women feel marginal and uncomfortable, and one of singles, where contacts may be limited and approaches, when they are made, may be predatory. Hite (1987) found those exiting from marriage often returned to inner-city apartments and joined the 'singles scene' that flourishes in that environment. These women were often reasserting the sexiness of adolescence or discovering sexuality for the first time, as sexual activity had atrophied in their failing marriages or had always been unsatisfactory. However, the establishment of a new sexual relationship may not be that easy or attractive for women who are no longer married. In his study of single parents, Weiss found that women engaged in masturbation and/or took a no-nonsense approach to their situation, where they dealt with sexual frustration by keeping themselves busy, and 'The strategy of keeping busy is easily adopted by a single parent whose normal state is overload' (1979, p. 206).

Although women without husbands may on average enjoy an improved sex life, there are variations. Many older women see themselves as past a sex life, and for widows the establishment of a new relationship may smack of disloyalty to their husband and hence be avoided. And even where disloyalty is not an issue there is a wariness and fear that a new person would be too similar to, or too different from, former partners. Other women, especially busy single parents, postpone developing a new relationship because they feel not ready, and are burdened enough. Their night-times may be taken up with putting the children to bed, and collapsing, and to fit a love affair into a busy schedule would be too much. There is anxiety that their bodies are not in mint condition, sagging rather than sexy, and that the men they meet are unsuitable or that there is something wrong with those who are available. Hite also reported that many women are horrified by the mores of casual sex, which still exudes a double standard, where men presume the availability and willingness of lone women, but simultaneously despise those who easily succumb to their blandishments. In this, widows and divorcees may be especially vulnerable, as being a long way removed from virginity they cannot be despoiled by further sexual activity and may be pressured into being obliging, if not grateful, for the continued sexual favours of men. For women who feel an obligation to control the sexuality of their children and set a moral example, there are difficulties in how open to be about new sexual partners. Also children, jealous of the new relationships, may strive to undermine them.

Finally, there is the problem of reputation. This presents dilemmas for lone wives and is an acute problem for those with absent husbands. Lone women may be urged to go out, meet people and enjoy themselves, but if they do they are seen as loose and accused of neglecting their children. Absent husbands were always anxious about their wives' fidelity and keen to restrict what they do in their absence and other women are keen to gossip about those alone. Although the issues are less ambiguous for women whose marriages have ended, the pejorative images continue to cling to their social activities and their relationships. The issue of reputation then pushes back many women into a safer and all-female world.

Conclusion

There is a heavy weight of literature concerned with how women experience and deal with lost relationships. Loss and absence is associated with poor mental and physical health and they are seen to present tasks for individual development and adaptation. However, here there are poor comparisons with women in conventional marriages, little acknowledgment of how models of lone women reflect assumptions about marriage, and no conceptual room for benefits of a life without marriage or domestic partnership.

While not denying the relevance of emotions an analysis which relies solely on this approach is limited to its vision. Reactions to loss are socially grounded – influencing what people feel and how they express their feelings. This moves the discussion from the emotions to the circumstances of the women. It sees the problems they experience not as personal and individual but related to the position of wives and women in the social order. It is to the social location of women without husbands that succeeding chapters turn and in the next chapter to their support structures and leisure patterns.

5

Support from family and friends

Partnership in marriage implies that husbands and wives support one another emotionally, economically and in the practical tasks of managing a joint household. This raises what appears to be simple question about whom, if anyone, women without husbands turn to when they are in need. The answer is more complex than the question, since there are epistemological issues of what constitutes support, how it is assessed and the adequacy of the support that is forthcoming. This is an area where there are mixed messages about general support for women inside conventional marriage, let alone those outside of it, where the extent and the types of support actually obtained from husbands is lost in an ideology of marital partnership. If the issue of support is framed in terms of finding a husband-equivalent, then women without husbands or spouse-like partners may, by default, seem to be obtaining less. Alternatively, if the support experienced by women without husbands is compared to actual levels of support experienced by married women, they may appear less disadvantaged.

One way of conceptualising society is to see it as an interweave of allegiances and obligations, and marriage alters women's participation in this interweave. On marriage women adopt a more domestic personality, becoming housewives, whether they are in paid employment or not. As housewives there is more pressure on them to make their homes, tend their hearths and cultivate their gardens, since marriage and parenthood continue to bind women firmly into the world of 'kinde' and 'kuche', if no longer 'kirche'. This private and domestic world influences the ways in which married women relate to other people. The question then becomes how far the disconnection of women from husbands influences these allegiances and obligations, the giving and receiving of social support.

It is against the changing basis of support in marriage that support outside marriage must be judged. There are suggestions that couple-based support is more important today than among earlier generations. Holme's study (1985) of young couples in East London notes the change since the more immediate post-war era recorded in *Family and Kinship in East London* (Young and Wilmott, 1962). In the modern metropolis people are no longer 'vigorously at home in the street', but secluded within their increasingly comfortable homes. Whether they were in the suburbs of Woodford or in the council flats of Bethnal Green, the young mothers Holme studied identified husbands as their prime source of support, both because wider kin were less available and because fatherhood was now defined as more active and participatory. 'In Bethnal Green husbands were mentioned as helpers and advisers as often as mothers. In Woodford husbands took top place for over half of the wives' (1985, p. 140). Where women have moved away from wider families it is not so much that the relationships between husband and wife are more symmetrical and the sharing more equal, but that couples are forced to be more reliant on one another in these circumstances, since if they do not rely on one another there is no one else to rely on. Also the involvement of husbands was regarded as significant despite the continuance of a traditional division of labour, where women shoulder the bulk of household chores.

In discussing the significance of pregnancy and childbirth for fathers, McKee (1982) notes that men are seen to contribute the 'spirit of support' to wives and the 'moral context' for childcare whatever their level of practical help. The particular emotional and moral context of conjugal support may mean that it cannot be qualitatively compared with the help forthcoming from other quarters. Men expect and are expected to be involved in child-rearing and entertainment if not household chores, and more may be expected of them in times of minor crises. Whatever their routine contributions to childcare, they are always seen as the parent in reserve. With assumptions of companionacy it is increasingly assumed that, when there is a problem, husbands will be the ones to step into the breach, which makes the question of what women do when husbands are not there more pressing. Discussing the support that women derive from husbands is a broader issue than whether or not they do the washing up, and the nature of support gained from other sources is complex and variable, ranging from emotional sustenance to practical help.

The support of friendship is different from that of practical help. The non-marital support discussed in much of the literature is based on specific research among the divorced, the widowed and the one-parent family and focuses on the stress of being alone and the problems of overload and pile-up, all created by the lack of a partner. More detailed comparative analyses of women with and without husband suggest a more complex picture. Tietjen (1985) found that women without husbands obtained more support from family and friends than those with husbands. The research assumes that husbands are supplying the additional support, but surveys of conventional marriage are more equivocal. There are many married women isolated in non-supportive relationships and some who are the victims of domestic violence and *require* support because of the nature of their domestic partnerships (Edwards, 1987).

Issues of support slide into general questions of community involvement, where support is two-way and women are both givers and receivers. The lack of someone to care for may be just as problematic as the lack of support itself and loneliness is a common experience among women without husbands. Women miss their husbands as someone to talk to and share affection with, and as someone with whom they can share household responsibility. They also miss their husbands as someone who structures their times and at least partially fills their day with tasks and activities. In his absence 'being busy' is given new meaning and takes diverse forms, ranging from outside employment, involvement in social activities and friendship groups and a more assiduous attention to house maintenance and childcare. In the absence of a husband, women's other relationships become extra important. Rubin (1983) has argued that women are more skilled at forming same sex friendships than men and feminist theory and research has emphasised the special and even superior qualities of these relationships.

Friends and family play an ambivalent part in support for women without husbands. The dissolution of a marriage disrupts and changes kinship and friendship networks, but family and friends are also important sources of informal support. These sources of support are characteristically assessed for their equivalence to an 'ideal' married relationship. In its baldest form the question is how far women without husbands find support elsewhere. McLanahan and colleagues (1981), however, argue that the support women do obtain from family and friends differs qualitatively. Hence any simple assessment of 'more or less', or 'better or worse', misses important qualitative differences in support for women and its varied social consequences.

Family support

Macfarlane (1986) has attempted to set the historical pattern of marriage in Britain within an anthropological framework. He argues that 'It is generally the case in other societies that after divorce or separation a woman is entitled to family support: she rejoins her kin group where she and her children may be welcome. Her dowry may revert to her' (p. 228). However, it would be wrong to assume that kinship networks and extended families always supply the safety net for women left on their own in Third World countries, especially when gripped by the forces of economic change. Here migratory labour and the seasonable absence of men are endemic economic processes, as in the southern parts of Africa, where industrialism joins hands with apartheid to produce towns of migrant men and homelands of women without husbands. Murray (1981) found that in Lesotho, two-thirds of the households were headed by women. The domestic economy of these women is dependent on cash remittances from migrant workers, and these often become infrequent or fizzle out altogether as men are exposed to urban spending patterns and form new partnerships. The myth of the extended African family is that kinsmen will substitute for absent or deserting men. However, Murray found that this was rarely the case and the women eked out a living largely unaided.

Macfarlane, having made a general anthropological point about traditional societies, goes on to say that, by contrast, 'the position in (historical) England seems less favourable. There was no kin group to return to: no brothers, parents or more distant kin had any responsibility to shelter or maintain her or her children. Marriage had cut the last strong links and she was alone' (ibid, p. 228). Similar comments could have been made about the widowed. The extent to which marriages are seen as entire and total is the extent to which their dissolution may leave women washed up on the shores of destitution and their position a social anomaly.

Commitment to marriage may be at variance with wider family ties. Women are broadly associated with care and their family involvement has a double aspect: they are seen as needing support, especially in their role as mothers, and as giving support to all members of the family, including the elderly and infirm. Classically mothers and daughters exchange these caring services (Lewis and Meredith, 1988; Ungerson, 1987), and where daughters are unavailable, daughters-in-law are substituted. There are then policy implications for the care of elderly relatives. Parker (1985) suggests that the bulk of today's single women are unlike their never-married counterparts in bygone years, being too busy or too poor to take on the additional burdens of caring for the elderly. Also cohabitation establishes weaker connections and obligations with kin than does conventional marriage.

However, when marriages end, there is some sense of returning to one's own family of origin and contacts with in-laws are often hard to sustain. Where a woman has not built strong and independent relationships with her husband's kin, connections wither with his departure and the removal of the kinship link. In Western kinship structure, in-law relations are generally problematic, evidenced in the uncertainty about what you call your in-laws and some tension as to how these relationships should be constituted (Wolfram, 1987). It is hardly surprising then that the ambiguity of in-law relationships should lead to the weakening or abandonment of these ties in marital dissolution. Divorce, particularly, provokes tugs of loyalty and the desire to apportion blame, which fracture links that are already more tenuous. Families feel obliged to support their 'own' and, in the desire for a clean break and a fresh start, ties with in-laws may be swept away. In-law relations are particularly vulnerable in divorce, but death also stirs anger in grief, removes the link person and wears away common ground.

Finch and Mason (1989) discuss the public morality of in-law relationships after divorce and individuals' accounts of their own relationships with in-laws. In their survey of family obligations there was a widespread consensus that, where relationships had been good during the marriage, these links should continue after its dissolution but, despite popular support for their continuance, few of the individuals surveyed about their own family connections had in fact continued them. The minority of cases where in-law relationships were sustained related to particular factors. These were: a long history of reciprocal support organised about women's responsibilities; a good relationship while the marriage lasted; a desire to facilitate grand-parenting and to find a new basis on which to continue the relationship; and the absence of a bitter struggle and recriminations during the divorce. In the cases cited by Finch and Mason the women sustained the relationship through the maintenance of 'as if' relationships, where contact was maintained with a mother-in-law 'as if' the marriage had not dissolved and sisters-in-law were equated with sisters. Central to the maintenance of the relationship was the continuance of reciprocity and in this way any continued relationship appears to imitate friendship, where the reciprocal nature of exchange is more central.

Strengthening links with families of origin is one way women deal with marital dissolution and single parenthood and this is particularly important in the provision of accommodation. For teenage unmarried mothers solutions are polarised. On the one hand some continue to live at home with their parents, making their dependency on kin greater and more prolonged than that of young women without children. Others may live separately and with limited contact with parents, especially if family relationships have been unsatisfactory. For older women a return to parents is a common but often temporary answer to marital dissolution. Sullivan (1986) and Burgoyne and Clark (1984) found that almost a third of divorced women returned at least initially to their parents' home. Here families continue to provide the ultimate safety net and a safe base from which individuals may more securely plan their future. The issue of housing for women without husbands is more fully discussed in Chapter 6.

However, even where there is not a physical moving back into a parental household, there may be a psychological reunion and this is strengthened by proximity. McLanahan, Wedemeyer and Adelberg (1981) found family networks for former wives small and intense and the contact frequent. In these family-based networks a few individuals were providing most of the support and the support that was forthcoming was gendered in stereotypical ways – fathers and brothers helped with household repairs and mothers and sisters with childcare. Although there was usually some reciprocity, relationships were asymmetrical, where the woman was reincorporated as the child of her parents and flow of services was in her favour.

There is a sense in which returning to the family of origin is turning the life-course clock back. For women without husbands, families contribute considerable amounts of direct services in childcare, house maintenance and housework and sometimes contribute financially. In the area of emotional support, families of origin gave individuals a sense of security, which many women interpreted as relieving them of the necessity to search immediately for another partner or husband. However, as this type of reintegration is that of the child with her parents, it has connotations of dependency and so the avenues for intimacy, and for a confiding and egalitarian relationship, are more limited. Although sisters may fill the gap, they only do so when they themselves are without husbands. Families of origin may supply immense practical help but limited understanding. They may even be preoccupied with maintaining the respectability of the women or, in their desire to 'help', err towards patronisation and smothering. The family provides a haven but one which also isolates women from wider community involvement, inhibits the development of new relationships and limits participation in social activities outside the family fold, and this is especially so if the women themselves have children. There are also areas in which the support of friends is no match for the duties of family. Where there is no continued relationship with fathers, single-parent mothers are often concerned about who would care for their children in the event of their own death or incapacity. In these circumstances the formal duties of guardianship devolve to families and here obligations are strong.

The different types of support offered by family and friends were made clear in a survey of naval wives (Chandler, 1987), women in husband-absent marriages. In assessing levels of support there was a graduation from mother through father and mother-in-law to father-in-law. Not only were in-laws less frequently mentioned but, when they were, their help was seen as on the scale of being moderate rather than considerable. Also emotional closeness to one's family appeared not to rely on physical proximity and daily contact, as many mentioned the telephone in supplying the vital link. Parents and parents-in-law featured more strongly in questions of practical help rather than companionship and the women showed no reliance on formal agencies or organisations either for companionship or practical help. Also over twice as many naval wives identified themselves as practically, rather than emotionally, isolated: one in seven relied on no one for help and one in fourteen relied on no one for friendship when their husbands were away. To underline the position of this minority, more claimed that they relied on no one 'a lot' rather than 'a little'. Such answers may not make sense grammatically, but they encapsulate a sense of independence and/or isolation. The 'other' category in 'sources of company' was dominated by 'myself', with dogs, cats, and canaries as runners-up. For 'other' sources of practical help, again 'myself' featured large, assisted this time by paid repair men.

Patterns of domestic support are particularly crucial when women without husbands are also caring for children, and to elucidate this, naval wives were asked who they looked to when they were temporarily incapacitated. They were asked who had helped during the time of the birth of their last child and, if they had children, who dealt with the household affairs when they were last ill in bed. Despite their intermittent absence, husbands dominated answers about the time of childbirth and even more so when women were confined to bed with illness: two-thirds of the women claimed assistance from their husband at the birth of their last child and 40 per cent some help from their mothers. Among women with children who had been recently bedfast with illness, nearly half were looked after by their husbands and a fifth by their mothers.

Again there is some indication that the importance of husbands at these times has increased in recent years. Nicholson's study (1980) of naval wives offers something of a historical comparison, since the fieldwork that forms the basis of this study was undertaken in 1971–2. In relation to childbirth, not only were husbands mentioned more frequently in the 1985 survey, but support from wider kin was less evident. A similar gap had appeared when the issue of illness was considered. In the 1971–2 data the wives resident on the married quarters estate investigated by Nicholson were receiving similar levels of support during illness from their own kin as from their husbands. When the 1985 data were examined stark differences appeared in the reported help from husbands and from kin; in 1985 husbands were identified nearly three times more often as giving assistance when wives were ill and bedfast as were their mothers.

The findings on childbirth and illness have a paradoxical side to them. They could denote the greater *involvement* of men in these events or indicate the greater *dependence* of women on their husbands as their prime source of support. Where women are still married, the issue appears to be one of balance between the inputs of husbands and wider kin rather than simple substitution, but, throughout, care given by a husband cannot be assumed to be qualitatively the same as that given by a mother, other relatives or friends. Also contemporary naval wives expressed a primary reliance on husbands despite their routine and regular absence. The anomalous claim may mean that these women were less supported than either those without husbands altogether or those conventionally married. Furthermore, to claim reliance on a husband who is largely not there suggests a growing gap between expectation and performance, feeding disappointment in marriage and leaving women tied to absent husbands and in reality more isolated and unsupported.

The literature on the level of family support for women without husbands dwells mainly on relatives of the same or older generation, but children also have a vital part to play, especially if support is seen as multi-dimensional. Naval wives identified their children as their mainstay companions and Weiss (1979) notes that, for many single parents, children may provide the major form of companionship and meaning in women's lives. Weiss found the children of lone mothers more involved in decisions and more aware of their mother's feelings. In single parenting there may be more opportunities for children, especially older ones, to take more responsibility within the household and towards younger children, and even to partially substitute for the absent parent.

Friends

Just as marital dissolution disrupts some kinship relationships and transforms others, so friendship networks also change. Women detached from husbands may have greater need for friends and greater opportunity to participate in friendship groups, but this must be undertaken outside the world of couples. The friends of women whose marriages have ended will often be new, and this is particularly marked in the case of divorce, where friends a woman has been closest to in marriage are those most likely to fade when marriage ends. Contacts are eroded by conflicts of loyalty in the dissolving partnership and the disappearance of the common ground of marriage and its expression in couple-based social activities. Women exiting from marriage often feel that their friends have deserted them and, even if the break is undramatic, they have to set about building a new social circle as single women.

McLanahan and colleagues (1981) describe an alternative to reliance on families of origin, as some women develop a looser-knit network of friends, mixed with relatives. Within this type of network female friends, and especially other single women, are prominent and, although the network may contain men, relationships with men are regarded as similar to relationships with women. In addition, there is greater participation in more formal organisations, also often women-based. Relationships in these friendship networks are less intense and more fleeting, reciprocal and *ad hoc*, in contrast to the more complete and obligatory notion of family support. The exchanges are less gendered with a greater range of services being supplied by other women. Reliance on friends is more favoured by middle-class women, whereas returning to family is more popular among those from the working class. Also, reliance on friends is associated with other attitudes, as those women who are keen to establish an independent status and career for themselves tend not to see single-parenthood in itself as problematic and are eager to participate in community organisations. These networks supply more emotional than practical support and are less secure than families as members come and go. Although membership of women's or single-parent groups may be transitory, it appears to supply vital socialisation into the new circumstance, plus role models and confidence.

Strengthening ties with family and friends may be an alternative, however temporary, to the establishment of a relationship with a new partner. In these models of networks each was supplying a different type of support, relating the women differently to the local community and fostering a different type of identity. However, it would be a mistake to see friends and family as only compensatory for the lack of a husband, as there are also glimpses of a new and alternative life outside conventional marriage. Here there has been interest in the development of women-based support networks, where other women are not simple substitutes for missing husbands. Also the feminist movement has put special store by the relationships formed between women, seeing them as the repository of what is good about the female, their sensitivity and nurturing qualities. But there is also a less pleasant side to female support. Orbach and Eichenbaum (1988) discuss the envy and competition that permeate women's friendships and limit the possibilities of a greater female solidarity. Also the sheer busy-ness of many women without husbands, especially those with children and in paid employment, reduces their ability to reciprocate, whatever their personal need for support themselves. Although there are difficulties with Orbach and Eichenbaum's discussion, as it relies heavily on psycho-dynamic models of behaviour and the women it discusses were those who had presented themselves for 'therapy', it does point out the blocks to fellow-feeling and the limited capacity of friends to supply support.

These issues are also pertinent to women with temporarily absent husbands. As in the McLanahan survey friends here give emotional support rather than practical help. A number of the naval wives interviewed (Chandler, 1987) stressed the necessity for outside contacts and many suggested that, with their husbands away, they had a greater opportunity to structure their own leisure time. As Finch (1983) has argued, the 'pattern [of periodic husband absence] may be one where it is easier to devise coping strategies, precisely because one's husband is sometimes completely out of the way. In these circumstances, wives are freer to devise strategies to meet the needs of their children and themselves, without having to take account of a husband's timetable on a day-to-day basis' (p. 69). Husbands do structure the daily lives of their wives, but even when they are not there women may not be able to escape wider patriarchal controls, controls exercised with particular force within the context of leisure, and women may be inhibited in forming deeper friendships.

Leisure activities are not sexually neutral. Women who want a social life, especially one active in the evenings in areas frequented by men, may encounter male hostility or predation (Whitehead, 1976). Also after marriage and/or with the birth of children nights out for women become fewer. In her study of women's leisure patterns, Deem (1987) found that the majority of married women in their twenties and thirties spend most of their time at home, kept there by housework and childcare and Glyptis and McInnes (1987) found that lone mothers had an even less active leisure life. In going out other women friends are essential in bolstering confidence and providing company and the extent to which women without husbands can support one another in sustaining a social life is raised as another important question.

Friends and neighbours

Thus far friendship has been treated in a largely unproblematic way, but it deserves a closer inspection. As Allan (1979) noted, friendship is a personal relationship in three important ways: it is a relationship between individuals; it is private; it involves a cultural construct of the person as they 'really are'. Friendship then appears highly idiosyncratic and individualistic, but is nevertheless socially structured. There is also vagueness about who friends are and distinctions are drawn between acquaintances, associates, neighbours and friends.

Abrams (Bulmer, 1986) adds to the discussion, arguing for a firm distinction between friends and neighbours since their linkage brings the unwarranted assumption that neighbours will be friendly, whereas in reality contacts with neighbours are either riven with hostility or kept cordial through a policy of distance or indifference. Abrams emphasises this distinction when he describes neighbouring as friendliness without the further involvement of friendship. The good neighbour is someone who helps and then withdraws, who establishes good relationships based on respect for privacy and reciprocity. Both Allan and Abrams see friendship and neighbouring as problematic. This is especially so for women whose domesticity makes the home a natural place for socialising. Here the rules of privacy invasion are more laxly applied, and where they survive, refer to the quality of the relationship rather than to physical distancing.

Neighbourliness takes place within a community context and McLanahan *et al.*'s study (1981) assumes a more loosely knit anonymous urban environment, but not all women without husbands live in these circumstances. Single mothers are often concentrated in cheap public housing in inner cities, where unsafe neighbourhoods confine them and their children to hours cooped up inside their flats (Hardey, 1989). Also many service wives live in the close community of married quarters accommodation. In service estates women are linked through the common occupation of their husbands, their homogeneity in terms of age and household structure and their limited ability to travel off the estate. They are communities in which friends and neighbours overlap and such an area can be seen as especially ripe for female fellowship and community action. In the study of naval wives (Chandler, 1987) many women had formed close friendships with their neighbours and were active in community centres promoting women- and children-based activities.

On the naval estates friendship among the lone wives could be very intense and took the form of shared meals, chats, coffees and help with childcare. As one woman said, 'You tend to live with each other, because, if your husbands are both away, everything every minute is "where are we going tomorrow? what are we doing tomorrow?".' The friendship groups rarely involved husbands and flourished only while husbands were away. There was also a group who rejected such close neighbouring, as other women were seen as always complaining and always borrowing, or these close networks were dismissed as a waste of time, a distraction from the more important business of housework and paid employment. Additionally there was an element of 'learning to befriend' when new wives discovered that they would have to spend much of their time on their own. They learnt 'to make an effort', for their own sanity, emotional survival and to enrich the lives of their children. However, bad experiences with neighbours also taught them caution and reserve.

Although lone naval wives may form a relatively close community, a closeness fostered by proximity and circumstance, intense neighbourliness was not seem as an unblemished good. Abrams (Bulmer, 1986) contrasts traditional neighbourliness with its modern forms, where geographical mobility, diversity and alternative services have created choice and social distance within localities. He is critical of close and closed forms, arguing that 'Most neighbourhoods today do not constrain their inhabitants into strongly-bonded relationships with one another. Those that do are either exceptional or regrettable' (p. 94). They are to be regretted for the personal costs invoved in intimate neighbourliness and the fierce social controls exercised by close communities.

Ross (1983) adds an historic dimension to the argument in her description of neighbouring relations among Victorian working-class London women. She describes them as survival networks, not as patterns of sociability. Here women that remained aloof also had to exist without the safety-net such links provided. The contemporary circumstances of many lone wives are less dire, the choices open to women broader, but the logic of such networks remains the same. Participation contains both costs and benefits; exchanges have to be reciprocated; networks are a force for local standards in appearance and behaviour; and 'Like all forms of intimacy, women's neighbouring relations generate tension and anger' (Ross, 1983, p. 15).

There is also a class dimension. Allan (1979), in his review of the literature of friendship, notes that working-class respondents consistently claim fewer friendships than their middle-class counterparts. These differences can be accounted for in the subtleties of class culture, where the middle class's apparent skill in sociability rests on their enthusiasm as 'joiners', their capacity to let relationships 'flower out' beyond their initial contexts and activities and a greater willingness to apply the term 'friend' more widely to one's social contacts. A further twist is added with the policies of urban renewal, the destruction of established working-class areas where locality and kin form the matrices of working-class sociability. With the erosion of traditional neighbours, 'Modern neighbourhoodism is in its purest form an attempt by newcomers to *create* a local social world' (Willmott, 1986, p. 95) and it is the middle classes who have the cultural predisposition towards such contemporary neighbourliness.

Estates dominated by lone wives are clearly an example of a modern neighbourhood, since there are no cumulative attachments of long residence or family ties and life there demands great skill in befriending and managing personal relationships. Naval wives with working class origins were much more likely to mention the problematic side of neighbour relations and had the most difficulty in managing those relations, and this was despite the fact that many had come to value the regular company of other women, the exchange of small services and inconsequential chatter (Chandler, 1987). Reciprocity is vital in relations with friends and neighbours and could be stretched to cover personal availability and accessibility, as well as services. Concern for reciprocity produces a wariness in relations and a fear of 'being used'. It also rests on similar standards and attitudes, and modern communities bring together women with different backgrounds with different expectations and standards and this can lead to antagonism and misunderstanding. Women without husbands can find themselves living in inner-city 'sink' estates and here there are status considerations in ensuring that the person you befriend is 'respectable', where it is important to comb carefully through potential friends and some reserve is necessary in order to be able to do this.

Lone women face a conundrum in their friendships. Distant relations may be hard to sustain and unsatisfying for those who seek a closer connection, but intense and more supportive ties can become overloaded and dissolve into bitterness and recrimination. Where relationships are closer and ostensibly more supportive, they are cliquish and gossipy, making groups hard to penetrate and alive with back-biting. In friendship networks women tend to develop best-friend relationships, but exclusivity in friendship creates avenues for triangular rivalries. Whitehead raises the issue of whether 'Female personal networks are indeed a potential basis for feminine solidarity and structures within which alternative ideologies can develop' (1976, p. 196). In her study she found little support for the proposition; the 'secret world of mothers and sisters' rarely took the part of a wife against a husband and so rarely do friends. Support for the married women is seen as interference and, for those no longer married, friends are often uneasy about their lone status and keen to encourage their remarriage.

Halem (1982) notes similar attitudes in the guides and self-help literature aimed at the divorced, where the term 'divorcee' applies largely to women. Women are the principal targets of self-help literature and much of it either describes the new situation as an erotic adventure or is full of cautionary tales about divorced women who have had bad experiences. She argues that the way in which divorce is seen oscillates between it being a uniformly painful or pleasurable state. Her conclusions apply as much to widows as divorcees and mark a discomfort in dealing with women's sexuality while retaining patriarchal assumptions about the nature of women and the control of their sexuality in marriage. Discussions of lone women demonstrate the retention and the redefinition of the double standard in contemporary society, as sustained by popular morality.

A teenage social life is predicated on having fun and on going out, but once women are in regular relationships or married, and especially if they have children, it is assumed that both they, and what could be construed as their leisure, will have become more home-centred. Where husbands are temporarily absent this has special force, but for those no longer married there is guilt and possible accusations of neglecting the children. Although women exiting from marriage return to a single state if they are mothers, the life-course clock is not simultaneously wound back and they are still regarded as quasi-married. For young single mothers it can however be wound forward, as childbirth brings a loss of teenage years. Adolescence is a time of non-responsibility but many single parents contend with employment, housework and childcare, when evenings may not be associated with fun but doing chores and watching television. Beyond the practical consideration of other commitments, to attend some venues without a male partner may be seen as odd or even disreputable.

Women whose marriages have ended often feel uncomfortable when socialising and this is no less so for those whose husbands are temporarily away. For this latter group a social life is confined to the safe daylight hours and involves only other women. Going out at night is redolent with the potentiality of sexual encounter and many dismiss this as too risky, both in the possibility of becoming involved with other men and because of what other women would say. And these risks limit the relationships between the women themselves, as they are concerned not to get involved in the sexual escapades of their neighbours and their plans to hoodwink husbands, and fear that invitations 'to go out with the girls' at night could lead on to other things. Hence most women with husbands away, like Penelope waiting for Odysseus spend their time tending their metaphorical looms and keeping other suitors at bay.

Conclusion

The obligations and assumptions of conjugality shape the support and friendship networks of all women, including those without husbands. They also create a background of meaning against which it is hard to assess and quantify the support women actually receive both in and out of marriage. Family, friends and neighbours are obvious candidates for supplying assistance and companionship, but as the relationships with each are different so is the support that is forthcoming. Also each contain their own potential problems – the smothering care of families of origin and the transience and politics of relations with friends and neighbours. These problems are often discussed for widows and divorcees, but they are no less pertinent for women whose husbands/partners are away.

All lone women have been seen as something of a moral threat and for centuries have been regarded with suspicion and this suspicion permeates their relationships. Absent husbands attempt to control their wives' fidelity by choosing their friends and limiting where they can go. For all, there is the problem that interaction in public settings often exaggerates the sexual element in relationships between men and women and is where women is regarded as fair game. Also the reputations of lone women may be assiduously scrutinised and guarded by other women and this reduces fellow-feeling and heightens suspicion.

6

Economic circumstances

A good marriage is widely regarded as offering companionship, affection and sexual satisfaction, main ingredients of human happiness. Such aspirations permeate the attitudes of young people on the verge of marriage and the approach of marriage counsellors and therapists as they aim to smooth out the wrinkles and deal with the shortcomings of marital relationships. As marriage is the intimate union of two individuals so its dissolution is tragic loss, and such thinking, popular and professional, tends to lead discussion towards the realm of the personal and psychological, with the financial and the bread-and-butter aspects of relationships pushed to one side in a concentration on the emotional.

Conventional family life also has an economic structure, delimiting separate but complementary spheres for husbands and wives, as breadwinners and homemakers. Here a wife exchanges domestic service for a husband's economic support and this remains the 'cardinal deal of married life' (Mansfield and Collard, 1988). These gendered priorities remain even when married women are in paid employment and husbands help around the home. The economic grounding of marriage is largely tacit and to discuss these issues openly is regarded as antithetic to the spirit of the relationship and even mercenary. However, when marriages dissolve and husbands are away, the economic foundations of the relationship are more clearly exposed and access to income and property become problematic.

There are a number of aspects to the economic circumstances of women without husbands. First, many women without husbands are poor and this is particularly true of mothers alone and the elderly. Second, the economic and welfare policies to which they are subject are rife with contradictions, for they are variously treated as self-sufficient workers and family dependants. Third, as their circumstances are complex so their sources of income are often diverse and interrelated. Finally, welfare policies towards women without husbands make moral and economic distinctions between different categories of women.

Lone women and female poverty

Lone women and single parents in Western society have always swelled the ranks of the poor and in recent years they have become the focus of debate about the feminisation of poverty. This trend refers both to the increase in female-headed households and the fact that these households are increasingly poor. Millar and Glendinning (1987) found, in their analysis of the 1983 Family Expenditure Survey, that there were two main types of household where income was likely to fall below 140 per cent of ordinary rates of supplementary benefit. These were those of elderly women living alone and of lone mothers: 61 per cent of these groups lived below what is conventionally taken to be the poverty line, compared with 28 per cent of all households, and together these two groups comprised a third of all poor households. The gap between the average income of one- and two-parent households is immense. In 1986 the total weekly income of one-parent households was less than 40 per cent that of two-parent households (National Council for One Parent Families, 1990).

Similar findings have emerged from the USA. Robins (1986) found that female-headed households had the highest poverty rates of any demographic group: 48 per cent of all female-headed households in the USA were poor, compared with 10 per cent of other types of households, and although a fifth were headed by women, they amounted to over half of all poor families. Within this group black women were over-represented since their lower rates of marriage and higher rates of marital dissolution mix with limited economic opportunities to generate material deprivation. Here instability in domestic relationships combines with class and colour to magnify the poverty of black women.

The poverty of these groups of women is, however, not new, as lone women have always been disproportionately poor, and not unique to the Western world. Historical descriptions of women in Europe are peppered with references to the plight of the deserted and the widowed and here discussion, as elsewhere, turns on the relationship between home and work, their control of economic resources and their rights to a living. In medieval society women had few independent economic rights, but their capacity to inherit from their husbands gave some widows a relatively privileged position. Analyses of the medieval economy in England reveal the economic independence of this group of landowning women; a study of ten manors in the Midlands 1350–1450 found that 14 per cent of the landowners were women and the great majority of these were widows (Shahar, 1983). The safeguarding of their property rights guaranteed them a living, while their once-married status rendered them immune from family interference or supervision and enabled many to resist the strong social pressures to remarry. Widows who controlled their own livelihoods enjoyed more freedom than any other type of woman in medieval society and prior to the Black Death, when land was in short supply, the widow of substance was viewed as a good catch in marriage. Work in other parts of the pre-industrial economy was based on the ownership of craft skills and controlled by guilds, many of which gave a widow the right to continue practising her husband's craft and even to train apprentices (Walby, 1986). She became the legal head of the family and her economic and social autonomy was publicly recognised.

With the development of capitalism women lost their access to skilled trades. Their productivity became confined to the home and their support became the responsibility of men, claimed for within the family wage. As working people became employees rather than masters or yeomen, and work moved from homes and outhouses into workshops and factories, so women, especially married women, were progressively excluded from these new forms of waged labour. These changes affected all women, including those ostensibly in the comfortable middle classes. Davidoff and Hall (1987) describe the growing dependence of women in the early years of the industrial revolution. In their analysis the new logic of business was connected to the transformation of the home, the former associated with the public world of men and the latter with the private and domestic world of women. Women were progressively excluded from the world of business and economic enterprise and their dependence in marriage was matched by investment strategies which maintained dependence even in widowhood. Where marriage conferred on husbands the rights to manage and control a wife's property and income, remarriage always posed a threat to a line of inheritance. To circumvent this, trusts for widows and children were established and these were run by male kin. Women were effectively given income from assets over which they had no control, and where they were permitted to run businesses it was only as a holding operation until sons matured and any rights that they had ceased on remarriage. Where women never married such trusts still prevailed.

As the assumptions of market individualism spread, sharp contradictions for widows emerged. While married, respectable women were to tend their families, but on their husband's death they were expected to support themselves, though not to become zealous business women, as flagrant ambition was seen to run against the grain of femininity. The difficulties of would-be entrepreneurs are illustrated in the area of farming. As 'farming became more rationalised and profit orientated, those landowners who had invested heavily in improvements sought tenants who would be "intelligent and enterprising", not the received stereotype of a widow' (ibid, p. 288). Landlords feared that lone women would not be able to manage or would fall prey to adventurers. Alternatively, with the strengthening definitions of feminine sensibility, landlords wished to save the woman alone from becoming an unseemly 'man in petticoats'. As the work of women was confined to the household and made only invisible contributions to the enterprise, so women without husbands became more dependent on men and more vulnerable.

For women of the less well-off and labouring classes the situation was even worse, as where women did not inherit their husbands' occupations they had to look either to employment or the charity list for their living. Historically widows were classified as amongst the 'miserabiles', to whom the church granted protection and alms. Using French data Tilly and Scott (1978) comment on the plight of less wealthy or fortunate widows. In Chateaudun the wives of vineyard owners gave up this occupation on their husband's death and became seamstresses and spinners. At least half the seamstresses and spinners listed on the tax rolls were widows and in eighteenth-century Bayeaux nearly half of all the textile workers in linen and woollen trades were widows. Their employment was sporadic, poorly skilled and low-paid. Where they failed to find work they, together with deserted wives and orphan children, dominated the poor lists.

In England, women were the major recipients of the New Poor Law introduced in 1834 (Thane, 1978), and among this group women without husbands were numerous. Within the Act women were seen as non-wage-earning dependants and there was limited recognition of, and provision for, those without a husband, especially if they were unmarried mothers or deserted wives. Poor Law guardians were always keen to distinguish the deserving from the undeserving poor and to ensure that financial help outside the workhouse (outdoor relief) only went to those destitute through no fault of their own. This meant that the able-bodied poor were subject to the more rigorous regime of the workhouse. This was designed to discipline work-shy men, and the status of fit women without husbands then represented a problem to the local boards and their treatment was subject to equivocation and local variation, especially as there were constant pressures to cut costs and eliminate outdoor relief.

Their treatment was also contingent on an assessment of their moral status. Widows were seen as the most deserving group and the one most likely to receive outdoor relief, although even here local boards would take some or all of the children into the workhouse to enable women to work. Deserted wives could not claim outdoor relief for a year following desertion as it was feared that greater generosity would encourage 'collusion' and lead men to renege on their responsibilities. Unmarried mothers received harsher treatment still. They were largely refused support outside the workhouse and life within the workhouse was organised for their moral correction. Successive reforms aimed both to encourage the able-bodied to work and to maintain the integrity of the family. When the relief was for women these aims were often incompatible, a problem which lingers in the present provision and regulation of welfare.

John (1980) also illustrates the position of lone women when she describes the historical ambivalence and debate that surrounded female miners and pit-brow workers in the last century. Women were seen as unfit for mine-work because it undermined their feminity and their capacity to be good mothers and homemakers. The arguments of the reform movement were tinged with a bourgeois philanthropy and a moral defence of the home and assumed that female mineworkers were conventionally married. Yet the majority were either single women, deserted wives or widows, driven to work by economic need and, for those who were the wives of ex-miners, by the necessity of retaining tenure of the colliery house. As protestations were made about the hardship that the exclusion of women from mine-work would cause, so extra money was added to male wages and more women without husbands ended up more reliant on charity and the workhouse.

Nevertheless the pressures for a family wage were often resisted and here the position of army wives, where the state is the paymaster, is a good example. Trustram (1984) in her description of military wives of the last century notes how port and regiment towns were filled with unsupported women and children as fleets and armies departed for foreign campaigns and imperial duties. The Victorian army restricted the number of soldiers permitted to be married, to limit its indirect responsibility for dependants. Wives in approved marriages were deemed to be 'living on the strength' and were entitled to barracks accommodation, rations and benefits, such as they were; in 1867, 7 per cent of men were allowed to marry, but there were of course many more wives living unrecognised in penury 'off the strength'. Trustram charts the arguments between public bodies and the military about who should take responsibility for these unauthorised dependants of military men and who should support them. Poor Law offered cold charity to this group, and this was especially so as it was progressively amended to make families more responsible for their dependants and husbands more economically liable for wives. As the Act reduced the local board's responsibility for destitute wives and the army tried to limit the payment of a family wage, so lone women were left to rely on their own resources.

These historical issues turn on the question of who should be responsible for women without husbands. In Western society wider kin has only a residual role to play in the economic support of lone women. If they are responsible for themselves and are treated as workers, then their economic survival depends on a sexually divided labour market. If they are economic dependants and the responsibility of others then their maintenance rests with men and the state, both of which have often been eager to limit their responsibilities in this direction. And there are other complexities. In their role as workers, employers assume that women are dependants, that paid employment is not their only means of support, and the female labour market is so structured; in their role as dependants it is assumed that women should, where they can, support themselves and maintenance is kept to a minimum so that economic self-sufficiency is not discouraged.

The following sections address this issue of economic responsibility, how it is structured and how the different bases of support for lone women are interrelated.

Access to male income and resources

Marriage for men brings the assumptions of breadwinning and for women their increased involvement in housework. As a companionate marriage emphasises commitment to this type of partnership, marriage commits women to prioritising their husband's job and to at least some financial dependence. What happens to this commitment when partnerships founder and are lost? There is some obligation on men to support women after death and divorce, but this has its limitations.

Women are twice as likely to lose their partners as men. Even in death men make a financial contribution to the support of their wives through inherited property, insurance schemes and entitlement to a pension. Hence, widows are often better off than their divorced or deserted counterparts. Nevertheless such benefits may not be long-lasting and elderly widows are among the poorest in the community and their relative poverty increases with age. Both Walker (1987) and Groves (1987) relate the poverty of elderly women to their reliance on pensions that are based on their husband's contributions and the inability of these women to build their own entitlement to an occupational pension. The post-war development of National Insurance, based upon a male pattern of earnings, made it financially unrealistic for most married women to accrue entitlement to their own pension rights; instead they were offered a married woman's option where entitlement was husband-derived. Private pensions were devised for only those in careers.

Dependence on a husband for a pension brings vulnerability to the vagaries of a husband's work record. The recession of the 1970s and 1980s added mass unemployment and redundancy to early retirement through sickness and injury, and increased the chances of people entering old age with depleted resources. Previously in

Britain the state has attempted to improve the income of the elderly and reduce their call on income support with the introduction of an earnings-related pension scheme. However, present policies aim to shed welfare responsibilities and limit expenditure on those that remain. The state earnings-related pension scheme has been curtailed as unacceptably expensive; it is proposed that women will inherit only half their husband's entitlement and that a smaller entitlement will accrue to those with lower and interrupted earnings.

By contrast recent private sector schemes have been more generous towards widows, especially if their husbands die while still in employment, and many of these private schemes do not expect widows to forfeit these pension rights if they remarry or cohabit. However, private pension schemes attach to better paid career jobs and only a minority of lone older women presently have entitlement to their own or a widow's occupational pension: in 1982, 40 per cent of lone women aged 60–64 and 37 per cent of lone women aged 65–69 were so entitled. An additional problem is the growing number of women who lose their pension rights on divorce or who maintain cohabiting relationships and therefore do not automatically acquire pension rights through their partnership.

Delphy (1984) argues that men have a continuing responsibility towards women beyond marriage. Separation and divorce are, in economic terms, marriage in another form, as women remain principally responsible for childcare and men continue to fund their maintenance. But, while the bulk of women remain committed to the economic relations of conventional marriage, divorce reform has largely eliminated obligations of their continued long-term maintenance.

Maintenance for women and children in the aftermath of marriage is an area of conflict. There is a clear obligation for fathers to support their immature children, but some ambiguity about how far this responsibility extends to mothers charged with the care of these children. The Matrimonial Causes Act of 1984 has sought to provide a clean break for adults whom, it was hoped, would walk away from their dissolved marriage as free and equal citizens. The courts' prime role in the dissolution has become the setting of post-marital arrangements, but these are organised less in terms of financial need and more in terms of capacity to pay and, only as far as the wife's behaviour is concerned, to reflect marital fault. With the exception of the matrimonial home, the court deals almost exclusively with income, and wider property and pension rights are largely ignored in the equation. With regard to income, maintenance payments are rare for childless women, small for lone mothers with dependent children or given only for a short and 'rehabilitative' period. Although there has been a greater recognition of the non-financial contribution that women make to the home, settlements have not yet gone as far as compensating women for the years that they have spent in this capacity (Joshi, 1987).

The General Household Survey estimates that until recently almost half of currently divorced women with children received some financial maintenance. However, Popay *et al*., (1983) estimates that only 6 per cent of lone mothers are reliant on maintenance from their former husbands as their main source of income and between 1981 and 1986 the proportion of lone parents on benefit who received maintenance fell from 50 per cent to 23 per cent (*Independent* 12 Aug 1990). Maclean (1987) adds to the picture. She found in her study of Oxford in the early 1980s that 'half [the maintenance awards] were below £10 a week, a quarter between £10 and £20 and only one quarter exceeded £20 a week' (p. 49). But although the sums were meagre they still formed a substantial part of the household revenue of these women, amounting to 'over a third of the household income for one in four of the recipient familes' (ibid, p. 49).

Maintenance payments are not only small, they are also often an irregular and unstable source of income. They are vulnerable to irregularities in the husband's work and his co-operation. Evason (1980) found in Northern Ireland that a third of her single-parent respondents claimed to receive maintenance payments irregularly but, as the amounts were small, lone mothers rarely pressed their claims through the courts. The situation is similar in the USA. Here, despite a child support enforcement programme for establishing paternity, locating absent parents and enforcing child support obligations, few women receiving welfare benefits obtained support from absent fathers. The Current Population Survey (1981, cited in Robins, 1986) found that 28 per cent of lone mothers claiming benefit had a formal child maintenance award and only 15 per cent were in receipt of such support. The additional problem of the unreliability of this form of income is that its nominal receipt may inhibit women from claiming additional state income support; here no maintenance at all may be a better circumstance than maintenance payments that are small and unreliable.

In recent years the numbers of lone parents in Britain in receipt of maintenance from ex-partners has fallen and has been associated with rising levels of social security expenditure. It has been calculated that between 1981 and 1988 the proportion of single parents on benefit rose from 38 per cent to 60 per cent (*The Independent*, 12 April 1990). The desire to cut welfare costs has linked with right-wing political opinion, keen that married and unmarried men should not abscond from their familial responsibilities, strengthening government's desire to pursue liable fathers. The state's capacity to enforce liability is harder where parents are unmarried. Collins (1990) has examined court decisions on maintenence payments where parents were not married. She found that women who had cohabited with the fathers of their children were much more likely to use the courts to secure maintenance and had been encouraged to do so by welfare agencies. However, most fathers were in low-waged jobs or unemployed and a number were supporting other children. These factors undermined any capacity to pay, ensured sums awarded were essentially nominal and that the bulk of cases were concerned with defaults and arrears rather than initial orders. As maintenance is deducted from benefits the actions of the courts make no contribution to the material improvement of single-parent households and the emphasis on paternal liability inhibits any serious consideration of this issue. As Collins states, the 'law impedes the development of the autonomy of single parent households, secures the dominance of the conjugal family and serves to reduce state spending on one parent families' (ibid, p. 21).

The continuance of marriage ties can also entail responsibility for debts. This is particularly important in relation to housing and its running costs. Taking over a mortgage or a council tenancy can include accepting responsibility for accrued arrears and this issue is also relevant when marriages have not ended but husbands are absent from home. Men who are away from home are not directly touched by the penury of their wives or the poverty of their children, and Evason (1980) notes that the debts of husband and household were a major issue with prisoners' wives.

Aside from income maintenance, the dissolution of marriage

involves a division of interests in the matrimonial home. Increasingly homes are jointly owned, but even when they are not, the Matrimonial Homes Act of 1967 gives the non-owning spouse the right of occupation. Where the property is sold, the division of rights is problematic. There is rarely enough equity in the matrimonial home to finance two houses and a growing divorce rate has led to pressure on the housing stock. Housing is an area where women without children do not necessarily fare better. Without dependent children, the property is more likely to be sold and the money divided, to yield a sum insufficient for the wife to buy another property. As a single person without children, she may be ineligible for a council property and the lower income of women means that she cannot with ease enter the private rented market or sustain a mortgage of any size. These problems of housing are more fully discussed later in the chapter.

As the law has changed to emphasise the contractual rather than the sacramental elements of marriage, there is the underlying assumption that the contract is formed between equals and that the rights of husbands and wives are interchangeable. Weitzman describes the situation in the United States where, in the move towards no-fault divorce, community property is often equally divided and the maintenance of divorced wives treated with diminished importance. 'The new rules for alimony, property, custody and child support all convey a new vision of independence for husbands and wives in marriages' (1985, p. 374). Yet the unintended consequence of such changes has been the growing poverty of divorced women and their children. Approximately one year after divorce the standard of living of divorced men had risen by 42 per cent, whereas the standard of living for divorced women had fallen by 73 per cent. Weitzman speculates that economic rationality may lead women to lessen their commitment to marriage as 'the new laws confer economic advantages on spouses who invest in themselves at the expense of the marital partnership' (ibid, p. 374). But to date there are few signs that this is happening. Her comparisons also assume that women when married had access to their partner's earnings, and this may not have been the case.

Burgoyne, Ormrod and Richards (1987) argue that Britain is moving towards a similar position, and echo the warning that marriage is not a contract of equals and its dissolution carries economic penalties for women and their children. Both Weitzman and Burgoyne and colleagues imply that it is dissolution that brings disadvantage. By contrast, Joshi (1987) suggests that women incur economic penalties while married and through their role as carers, and not through marital dissolution. If their marriage then dissolves these penalties are more manifest, as at that point they lose any compensatory access they had to a husband's earnings. As income support from husbands is a limited and an increasingly diminishing option, the new aim is economic self-sufficiency for women outside marriage where women are able to derive a greater proportion of their income from employment and build up their own entitlements to pensions and benefits.

Employment

Martin and Roberts's study (1984) of the employment careers of women found that lone mothers were in paid employment in the same proportion as married women. However, those with jobs were much more likely to be working full-time rather than in part-time and their motivations for working were different. They were much more inclined to regard their employment as paying for basic necessities, rather than family extras. On the face of it, these bald figures suggest that economic self-sufficiency is a reality for a substantial number of lone mothers. However, the numbers employed conceal a deep inequality as women seek a living in a gender-divided labour market. Women find work within limited spheres, where female jobs are poorly paid and insecure, and they characteristically experience downward mobility in the job market when they resume paid work after a break. In manual jobs a woman earns on average two-thirds of the male wage and, among the semi- and unskilled, low wages necessitate there being two earners in the household if poverty is to be kept at bay.

The economic circumstances of women without husbands is mediated by class, and whether women's class is derived from the economic position of men to whom they are/were connected or assessed on income and resources, they appear economically disadvantaged. The limited rewards for female work reduce the earning power of working-class women, and their middle-class counterparts, who may have left a career to care for children, are not immune from these disabilities. On divorce women married to middle-class men may be as vulnerable as those with working-class partners. Only if they themselves are in well-paid careers may they be able to sustain a reasonable standard of living for themselves and their children. These women are social rarities and most find themselves on or below the breadline.

The emphasis on economic self-reliance not only assumes that men and women are similar units in the labour market but that they have comparable types of family involvement. They do not. Women retain prime responsibility for childcare and this responsibility is a hidden cost to employment. Without extensive childcare support it is hard to sustain the full-time employment that is necessary to raise lone mothers' incomes beyond state benefit thresholds and make any employment worthwhile. The cleft stick becomes obvious when, in the absence of state nursery facilities, women have to earn a considerable income to pay for the childcare which enables them to be gainfully employed.

Where childcare has been provided it has sometimes included an additional sting in its tail that smacks of state coercion: in Poor Law Britain children would be taken to the workhouse to free their widowed or deserted mothers for employment; in '22 states in the USA single mothers drawing "workfare" must now put their children into daycare and work for their benefits' (Nathan, quoted in Lewis and Piachaud, 1987). Support for childcare for lone women is always tempered by the state's concern not to disadvantage those presently engaged in whole-time childcare. Such support may be more forthcoming in the future if there are labour shortages and single parents are seen as an unnecessary drain on the treasury coffers. But at present the barriers to employment – a frequent fall in real income, the high cost of childcare, the unavailability of suitable childcare and suitable paid work, and the absence of wider support for women in the care of their children – remain as high as ever (National Council for One Parent Families, 1990). Finally, for those women who do single-handedly support and care for a family, there is a personal cost. As one young widow commented, 'Eat, sleep, work; that's my life' (Evason, 1980). Such women are doing it all, and small wages buy little in the way of home maintenance or help with domestic chores.

Despite the objectives of encouraging more lone mothers into jobs, their participation in paid employment has fallen over the past decade in Britain: in 1976–8, 47 per cent of lone mothers were in paid work; by 1982–4 this proportion had fallen to 39 per cent (OPCS, 89). Recession has raised levels of unemployment. Economic restructuring has led to the polarisation of income groups as the wages of those employed in semi- and unskilled work have fallen or have failed to grow (Walker and Walker, 1986) and because of the casualisation of many jobs in the secondary labour market, particularly those performed by women. The substantial sums needed to lift lone women out of poverty are unobtainable by most and they find themselves working for little more than benefit levels. Among the lone mothers who formed part of a Family Finances Survey, 'of the 10% who took part-time jobs during the subsequent year, 71% still had incomes below the poverty line. Of the 4% who took full-time jobs, 37% remained below the poverty line. This means that for 62% of the women who took employment this gave little or no improvement on their supplementary benefit incomes' (Millar, 1987, p. 166).

Lone mothers in Britain have lower rates of labour market participation than in the USA or the rest of Europe and, within this category of women, unmarried mothers have the lowest rates of employment of all. Dex and Shaw (1988) suggest that women in the USA are helped to work by the tax relief available for childcare costs. The National Council for One Parent Families (1984) argues that the much higher proportion of 86 per cent of Swedish lone mothers are able to participate in paid employment because of improved working conditions and leave for parents. Also better treatment for part-time workers and childcare facilities make employment there a more realistic and rewarded option. These comparisons suggest that it is more not less help for lone parents that promotes their financial self-reliance.

Housing

Women without husbands suffer a major disadvantage in the housing market. They commonly move on the dissolution of marriage, have problems securing and keeping accommodation and are housed in poorer conditions. Housing circumstances are variable between sub-groups. Widows are the most likely to remain in their homes, although some still move, typically because they have difficulty with mortgage payments or because their existing accommodation is tied to their husband's employment. Nearly half of the women who are divorced move from the marital home (Sullivan, 1986), a proportion which rises substantially when the women are in the younger age groups. The presence of children, despite court policy appears to be a marginal factor, as 41 per cent of women with children move at this time. Similarly the class position of the husband has little impact on whether women move or not, but the economic position of new partners, together with the resources of the women themselves, are crucial in influencing the subsequent housing careers of the women.

As cohabitants women have fewer rights. Logan (1987) argues that only if women have children, whose housing needs are prioritised by courts and local authorities, do they acquire *de facto* the rights of the married. For those who are childless, family law is rarely applied and their housing rights approached with the general principles of property law or even the assumptions of landlord and tenant. Tenure type however is important. Women resident in privately rented accommodation are the most insecure and those in local authority housing the least likely to move following the dissolution of their marriage. Maclean (1987) found that few divorcees who were owner-occupiers were able to shoulder the full mortgage alone or to leave with enough equity to buy another property and fewer still moved on to subsequent owner-occupation.

The moves that are made on dissolution are often not once-and-for-all moves. Sullivan (1986) found that more than a quarter of divorced women had moved at least twice in the year following the divorce. Evason (1980) confirms the general picture in data gathered in Northern Ireland as she found that three-quarters of divorced women and over half of the separated had moved since the breakdown of their marriage and many had moved twice. Typically women move first to relatives and then into other accommodation, which they frequently have to furnish from scratch. In order to buy or privately rent accommodation women must have the necessary financial resources and many do not. The group for whom shared accommodation is less transitional are unmarried mothers, and only 40 per cent of this group form an independent household.

In Britain public policy offers lone women with children the chance of an independent life. But to be housed in public sector accommodation women must fulfil the policy priorities of local authorities. Principally they must have children, and women on their own frequently face considerable difficulty in securing accommodation in this sector. The importance of public housing is seen in the accommodation profile of one-parent households: in 1985, 61 per cent of one-parent households were in rented accommodation, including 55 per cent of those who were renting from the local authority. This compares with 25 per cent of households comprised of two parents and two children, of which 22 per cent rented from the local authority. Conversely a third of one-parent households were owner-occupiers, compared with three-quarters of households comprised of a couple and two children (Family Expenditure Survey, 1985). The only way in which women, once they have moved out of owner-occupation, can forestall entry into local authority housing and recoup their earlier position is to form a fresh partnership, to become once more a couple-based household.

However, even a sympathetic public housing policy does not prevent many women with children experiencing homelessness. For women who enter refuges this is a particular problem (Binney, Harkell and Nixon, 1985). Women suffering violence find it hardest to leave the marital home and, those that do, face immense problems in finding any other type of accommodation. They are rarely rehoused from a violent home and, if they have made themselves homeless, they encounter pressures to return. Court orders to exclude violent men from their own home are hard to obtain and even harder to enforce. Again those without children suffer a greater personal disadvantage.

State income support

Lone women, especially mothers with dependent children, and the elderly, are heavily reliant on state welfare; over half of lone mothers and a third of pensionable widows are in receipt of income support (Martin and Roberts, 1984; Walker, 1987). This support is nevertheless not without its problems and ambiguities. The welfare system assumes that people live in conventional families, that men are whole-time earners and women primarily homemakers. Hence entitlements to relief and benefits accrue either during whole-time uninterrupted paid employment – and here women can only achieve entitlement if they exhibit the same type of work patterns as men – or through the contributions of partners. For many women it is largely through their partners that they key themselves into the welfare system.

Although current thinking is keen to encourage women outside marriage to earn their own keep, the welfare system still opts to treat women primarily as mothers and dependents and not as workers. Lone mothers are permitted to be long-term claimants, are released from the obligation to hold themselves in readiness for work as a condition of benefit receipt, receive an additional child benefit allowance and are allowed to earn small amounts before this is removed pound for pound from their benefits. But there is ambiguity as, on the one hand they are encouraged to engage in a limited amount of part-time work, and on the other the benefit system assumes that people are 'unambiguously in full-time work or out of work; the needs of the part-time worker are virtually ignored' (Millar, 1987, p. 174). The system forces women to choose between employment and state support and presently more are opting for state support.

From Poor Law days rules of less eligibility have shaped the distribution of relief. There has always been concern to distinguish between the deserving and the undeserving poor and to discipline those who wantonly become destitute. Similar principals differentiate the treatment of different types of women without husbands. Widows receive more favourable financial treatment than the separated and divorced. They receive benefits that are taxed but not means-tested. Widowhood is seen as an entirely involuntary and legitimate misfortune and one against which their husbands have contributed in national and private insurance. Benefits for widows are not zero-summed with their earnings and there is greater encouragement, in policy terms, for them to participate in paid employment.

Benefit levels for men are set to encourage them to work. For women without husbands they are set to encourage their establishment of partnerships and marriage/remarriage. This influences the levels and policing of benefit, and when a liable man can be found or when women marry or remarry, the state withdraws its support. Widows Allowance is graduated and the graduation is an assessment of their marriageability as based on their age, benefits ceasing on marriage or cohabitation. The state regulates financial arrangements in divorce and separation and seeks to minimise its financial responsibility. The state checks the love-lives of women receiving financial support and in the USA pursues men attempting to escape from what are seen as their familial responsibilities. These rules of dependence can run counter to the reality of relationships between men and women and some strange anomalies occur. Lynes (1986) quotes the case of a single woman resident with and caring for a disabled man. Her benefit was withdrawn as, in the eyes of the state, cohabitation meant that she had become his financial responsibility. Benefits are set at a level to encourage women to become and remain married and, in the event of marital dissolution, to remarry or establish a marriage-like relationship.

Welfare and employment are, however, not simple alternatives. There are other complications. Being the recipient of state income support brings entitlement to other types of benefit, whereas eligibility for a family credit, an income boost for low wage earners, is only available to those in employment. The composite and complex trade-offs of income options make rational economic choice impossible for many women without husbands and many are locked into the tightest of poverty traps (Bradshaw, 1989). There are personal costs as well: 'living off the social' is demeaning and often time-consuming when giros go astray; full benefits have to be argued for and emergency loans wrested from cash-limited agencies.

Support from kin

In Western society marriage ideally forms the couple into an independent household. As it cuts links with families of origin there is no clear obligation for families to assist when marriages dissolve. Although women are rarely fully reincorporated into the family of their childhood, kin offer a wide range of general support to women without husbands and this support has an economic aspect. They offer temporary accommodation, small loans and services that facilitate paid employment. Gerstel (1988) found that families gave limited financial support, and Evason (1980) found that a third of single parents in Northern Ireland reported that they received some economic support from kin or friends, but what was forthcoming was small, intermittent and unpredictable. One crucial area where help was vital was in relation to childcare; among the mothers who were in paid employment, over half relied on the unpaid services of friends and relatives to achieve this. Kinship support aids employment and Gerstel also argues that the practical support of relatives helps forestall any drop into depression and despair. A more wide-ranging discussion of family support for lone women is found in Chapter 5.

Marriage alters kin ties, but marital dissolution weakens and disrupts them. Individuals may look more to their families of origin when other avenues of support present in former marriages become closed off. This is particulary so with an acrimonious divorce or separation where kith and kin fracture into sides. But death also changes the strength of kinship connection and may undermine the provision of services and financial help.

Implications

This discussion opened with the question of who is responsible for women without husbands. The obvious answer is women themselves, but their situation is so structured that it is not easy for them to be economically self-reliant. A model where all adults stand firmly on their own economic feet is not gender-neutral, but based on the experiences of men and at odds with the social forces that shape most women's lives. It ignores the role of women as the main carers of children, their interrupted work patterns and the disabilities of the female labour market. Also the income of female-headed households frequently derives from many sources, with a complex relationship between the different elements of which it is comprised. Welfare benefits may be an amalgam of piecemeal allowances and are often zero-summed with other financial resources. Women who are in paid employment may be working to earn only the same or slightly more than their benefit entitlement. Alternatively, other elements of economic support may be unrelated or even mutually supportive, as in kin support for childcare and employment. From her work on women in refuges Pahl (1985) regards their economic circumstances as less a matter of composite income and more 'a three-sided trap'. These women are caught between an unreliable and violent husband, the suspicion and indifference of social security and the difficulties of low-paid employment.

There are a number of economic consequences that flow from this complex economic equation. First, fewer lone women with dependent children are presently in paid employment, despite current thinking on its desirability. Second, the low pay of women and the restrictions on benefit receipt perpetuate the poverty of lone women, the visible portion of female poverty. Third, the issues do not solely relate to lone mothers with young children or a brief time in these women's lives. Their present income may not be greatly improved by employment but, taking the longer view, welfare income falls as children mature and women must eventually seek their living in the female job market. Again delayed entry into the labour market prejudices the acquisition of pension rights and generates the poverty of women in old age.

Familism is a structure pervasive and deep-rooted in Western society, a social thread in all gendered situations, and the best economic option for most women whose relationships with men have ended is remarriage or the establishment of fresh partnerships. Poor households require one-and-a-half if not two incomes to stay economically afloat. If part of the income is supplied by a man rather than the state, women can earn with impunity. When a group of lone women were re-interviewed after the space of a year it was found that those who had established new relationships had more than four times the chance of crossing the poverty line (Millar, 1987); Eekelaar and Maclean (1986) found that after divorce only 21 per cent of lone mothers had incomes greater than they would be entitled to on supplementary benefit, compared with 70 per cent of women who had entered fresh relationships. Aside from social and emotional considerations women are encouraged to remarry or cohabit on economic grounds alone.

The situation of women without husbands is economically ambiguous where women subsist on a complex composite income and can find themselves falling between numerous stools. Yet, despite the diversity of sources of income for many women without husbands, there are often impenetrable ceilings on their overall incomes. Few are well-off; the wealthy widow, the alimony drone and the high-earning single parent are rare and owe more to fantasy than fact. Many survive on the threshold of poverty and some are sucked down into a vortex of disadvantage from which they and their children find it hard to escape. On all objective measures, women without husbands are over-represented amongst the poor and subjectively financial worries top their list of major concerns. Evason (1980) found that 36 per cent of the single parents she interviewed in Northern Ireland were worried about money, compared to the 13 per cent who worried about children and the 4 per cent who were anxious about coping on their own. For elderly widows, eking out their pension is often the main preoccupation of their day. Practical problems of subsistence are uppermost in their minds as much as the loneliness of being on their own (Bowling and Cartwright, 1982).

Some reservations

The diminished economic circumstances of women outside marriage could be regarded as illusory and the comparison of circumstances in and outside marriage a false one. The ideological strength of 'the family' leads commentators to regard alternative household arrangements as odd or inadequate and to gloss over or ignore the shortcomings of conventional families. In normal families women are assumed to be benefiting from the overall household income, but Pahl (1984) and Wilson (1987) have described the uneven distribution of resources within households, a distribution which disadvantages women. Hence the poverty of women within marriage is largely invisible, yet it can be glimpsed in the comments of women no longer in married relationships. Evason (1980) argues that becoming a single parent is not an automatic move from 'adequacy to penury', since she found that 47 per cent of the divorced women, 41 per cent of the separated and 39 per cent of the widowed in her study claimed to be in the same financial situation or a little better off once their marriages had ceased, despite the fact that 70 per cent of the sample of women were judged to be living on or below the poverty line. Analyses of the economic circumstances of lone women may say more about the visibility of female poverty than its incidence.

So far the disadvantages and anomalous status of female-headed households have been examined in terms of a culture which assumes families will take a conventional nuclear form. However, there are sections of society where matrifocal families are more the norm and these are exemplified in the black American and Caribbean family. In Thorogood's (1987) study of black women in West London, 31 per cent were in female-headed households, and even where men were present, women were rarely wholly dependent on them for their livelihood. This suggests that black women are less married than their white counterparts and they wield greater authority in the family whether the husband is present or not. The black women interviewed were equivocal in their assessment of the costs and benefits of living with a man: men increased women's domestic labour as men required looking after and diminished their control of the household purse and time they had to themselves; husbands discouraged women from working and therefore also reduced their earnings. Such reasoning often lay behind the preference for separate accommodation and the reticence about marriage.

Thorogood relates this structure and logic to the black community, but its ethnic basis should not be over-stressed. Young white single mothers may exhibit a similar reticence to marry, even when they are in stable relationships. Young men who had failed to obtain a secure toe-hold in the labour market were seen as a poor marital option; the traditional view that marriage is only for the economically established seems to prevail.

Conclusion

The economic exchange of income and services and the establishment of property and pension rights are central to marriage. The absence of a husband creates visible benefits and penalties for women no longer married. Considerable evidence has been collected on the poverty of women without husbands, and within this broad category particular groups have been seen to be at greatest risk. These are mothers with young dependent children and the elderly widowed and divorced. There is considerable international variation in their treatment. Sweden has a long history of low marriage rates and high rates of non-marital cohabitation and family dissolution. Here the state makes more generous provision for one-parent families and does not financially penalise those with paid employment. The approach in the United States and Australia has been somewhat different. Here there are residual state benefits and workfare programmes, where the paid employment of women has been encouraged, and although the liability of men for former wives has been reduced, more rigorous attempts are made to enforce support payments for children.

There is evidence that the present position of many women without husbands has worsened. Present divorce policy has sought to produce cleaner breaks for couples when their marriages are dissolved and to reduce the claims of women for long-term alimony. Few women are supported by former husbands and the pensions for many elderly women are meagre. Large numbers of single parents subsist on a composite and sometimes irregular income and the complex relationship between income elements produces an income ceiling above which many women find it hard to rise. Benefit rules limit the extent to which women can combine income support and employment and the numbers of lone women in paid employment has fallen. As economic change has reduced the wages of many women and casualised their position in numerous workplaces, and despite the pursuit of liable fathers, more in Britain have opted to rely primarily on the state. Many improve their economic circumstances only by the establishment of a new relationship with a man and economic necessity may drive women into ill-considered liaisons with men which bring other costs for themselves and their children. Furthermore, an ageing population is seen increasingly in government circles as an economic burden and the state has sought to limit its financial responsibility in this direction. As the provision of an adequate pension is devolved more to private organisations, so a woman must imitate the career pattern of a man to become eligible, or remain married to a man with a pension which he can sustain and which she can inherit.

Changing attitudes towards marriage and the financial status of women could be said to reflect the increased numbers of women who are in single-parent households, or who cohabit, and even the increased numbers of longer-living elderly widows. But such a view is over-simplistic and over-optimistic. Both the position of women in the home and the structure of the labour market ensure the continued dependence of women on men and that marriage remains women's 'best career'. Women without husbands subsist in the long economic shadow cast by marriage and this reduces their income and their resources. The dissolution of marriage contains economic costs for women and these are allied to favouring conventional families and privileging men. As Barrett and McIntosh (1982) argue, 'the iniquities of the family and its appeal are closely related – they are two sides of the same coin. The benefits of family life depend upon the suffering of those who are excluded' (p. 133).

The discussion has emphasised the bleaker side of the lives of women without husbands. There is another side to their domestic economy and one that is hinted at in the analysis of the black Caribbean and American household. This relates not to the monetary resources they have at their disposal, but the less tangible issues of the management and servicing of the household. Absence of a husband not only affects the size and the composition of the household budget, it gives women tighter control on what they do receive and how it is spent. The absence of men from the household affects decision-making, housework and house-maintenance. Here discussion moves more from the receipt of income to the control of its expenditure and these issues form the basis of the next chapter.

7

Household routines and domestic power

Women without husbands live in households whose structures and routines differ from those of women who are conventionally married. Their family relationships, and those of their children, more obviously cross-cut household boundaries. The organisation of 'home' and the meanings that attach to it are also different. The absence of a husband releases women from the ties of a husband-centred schedule, enhancing their powers of domestic control but involving them in greater domestic responsibility. It also transforms the fine detail of domestic routine in which family life is reproduced. The experiences of women in this area vary with the context and dynamics of husband absence and their examination adds to our wider understanding of family relationships.

Household and families

Discussions about families in the West are often riddled with ambiguity about what is meant by the term 'the family'. The term is applied to both households and kinship relationships. The concept of the nuclear family integrates parenting and marriage, draws a clear boundary around the conjugal couple and their children and seeks to equate family with household. However, for many women without husbands, and especially for those with dependent children, aspects of family life diverge rather than converge. Divorce divides the relationship of parenting from that of marriage and where there is joint custody some responsibility for children is given to individuals resident outside the household. Hence, in the case of divorce and separation families are more obviously distinct from households. The frequent need to consult with a former spouse and the visiting patterns of children mean that household boundaries are permeable (Burgoyne and Clark, 1984) and joint custody arrangements may enable non-resident husbands/fathers to exercise some control over the lives of women and children (Brophy, 1989). Money, as well as individuals, crosses boundaries as, where child maintenance is being paid, household budgets are contributed to by non-residential family members. Families have political undercurrents, with scope for alliances, lobbying and disputes, and these are more manifest and more complex when families do not live under a single roof. There is a gendered uniformity in the households that are formed as marriages dissolve. As families divide, nine out of ten children remain with their mothers, creating lone mothers and absent-father households.

Ahrons and Rodgers (1987) explore the family structures of the divorced and separated. They argue that the term 'single parent family' is based on a central misconception. They challenge the assumptions that residence determines interaction, that in normal families the father will be active and involved with the children and where he is not resident he will not be active. They see the involvement of the absent father as a question of degree. But active fathering is rarely the same as active mothering. Fathers may continue contact with children and retain a right of veto, while not being central to their daily care.

Nevertheless the term 'single-parent family' is a poor descriptor since it implies not only that the unmarried have no partners but that absent partners are always uninvolved in family life. Rather, domestic relationships are formed in single-parent *households* but multi-parent *families*, especially where former partners have entered new relationships. As households divide and recombine, patterns of relationship become more complex and decisions about who is in and out of the family vary with the different perspectives of each family member. In an attempt to resolve this, Ahrons and Rodgers devised the term 'binuclear' families, which examines family structures from the viewpoint of the child who moves between them. While partly accepting their critique, the concept of 'binuclearity' is less than helpful, since it remains premised on the solidity of nuclear families, but suggests that there are two of them. They continue to see families as units rather than fluid – and not always coherent – sets of relationships. This is evident when household members are asked to identify their families, since parents often omit non-residential children and children do not always include step-parents.

By contrast, Weitzman (1985) argues that these changes in family formation and co-parenting have been more apparent than real. Similar relationships are now differently labelled, as what was regarded as liberal visitation is now called joint custody. This may have important psychological consequences for fathers and may encourage the retention of ties with their children, but it has done little to alter their living arrangements. Franks (1988) argues that the complexity of relationships between kinship and household that follows when marriages dissolve and new relationships are formed offers scope for more imaginative relationships and supports between people, but she also admits that the possibilities for creativity in family relationships rarely come to fruition. Consequently ties beyond the household are vulnerable and fraught with tension and contact with absent father–husband tends to steadily diminish over time.

Most discussion focuses on the links between the child and the absent parent, and the on-going relationship between spouses is rarely discussed or studied. There is a lack of language for these connections. And creating secure new relationships encourages the erosion of former and outside ties. Ahrons and Rodgers (1987) however, addressed this as an empirical issue. They found that nearly six out of ten separated and divorced couples did have stereotypically little relationship – here contact was rare and when it occurred it was focused on the children. The remainder had a 'declined' relationship with moderate interaction, exchange of information and some friendship, and these declined relationships varied from those of 'perfect pals' to those of 'fiery foes'. Both extremes of the relationship were hard to sustain over time as old attachments and burning resentments tend to fade. High levels of openness and co-operation were seen as impractical, especially as new relationships were formed and privacy increasingly valued. It was not just the couple themselves who determined the quality of the relationship. High levels of co-operation between former spouses generated ambivalence in others, and where an on-going relationship was retained this was seen as pathological or odd.

There are also other aspects of household complexity as single mothers are reincorporated into the households of their parents or, having a child, are discouraged from leaving the families of origin. Marital dissolution is associated with housing difficulties and kin often supply necessary but temporary accommodation (Sullivan, 1986).

Despite the atypical structuring of households, the ideology of the family is powerful. The desire to be like an ordinary family can lead people to tighten household boundaries and to weaken ties with non-residential members. Also husbands who come and go from families create some ambiguity about who is in and who is out of the family and what their place is within the home. These issues re-emerge in the chapter on reconstituting family life.

Housework and homemaking

Marriage absorbs the time and energy of women in housework and much of this derives from the servicing of men. In conventional marriage domestic routines are fitted around male schedules and career patterns. The absence of men or marriage may mean less housework and offer women more domestic control and at the very least it will change domestic routines. Lone women's control of the household is theoretically uncontested, since there is no partner with whom to bargain or to whom to turn for support, but this is an empirical question and one that relates to the amount of control women comparatively exercise in and out of marriage.

In a pre-feminist era it was accepted that women's power in public life was restricted, but women who controlled domestic decision-making were viewed as matriarchal. However, more recently the nature of women's power in the household has been questioned. Their minor decision-making in the home has been distinguished from the major decision-making of men, or responsibility for housework or childcare is not seen as power at all. Distinctions have been drawn between the big and rarely made decisions that set the tone and contours of family life, which are the prerogative of men, and the small and regular decisions that are the stuff of everyday living and the province of women. Men are seen as having the power of orchestration and women the time-consuming duties of implementation. Even where there is no obvious choosing, husbands maintain a veto and wives exercise delegated power only so long as their decisions fall within guidelines predetermined by husbands (Edgell, 1980; Mansfield and Collard, 1988). Modern marriage, where men are expected to take a more active interest in the home, may even have diminished the domestic powers that women traditionally exercised.

There are, however, some difficulties with this argument relevant to women both in and out of marriage. First, household chores are defined in a narrow, female-derived way which can limit empirical enquiry into men's contribution and the domestic implications of their absence. Second, gender creates an optical illusion which distorts discussion of domestic power and big and little decision-making. Imray and Middleton (1983) argue that it is not that some social activities are intrinsically and accidentally both female and trivial, but that what women do tends to be trivialised; conversely it is not that men engage in activities that are intrinsically male and socially important, but men endow what they do with kudos and social importance.

Third, there are arguments for the cultural centrality of housework. Douglas (1970; 1972) regarded the housewife as the main agent for identifying and transforming the dirt and chaos of the natural world into the cleanliness and the order of the cultural world. In the organisation of time, space and matter, housewives construct meals and schedule mealtimes. Martin (1984) furthers the argument, warning against accepting and repeating the wider societal verdict that housework is trivial. For Martin, housework is central to the creation of social existence as it is 'a cultural practice of great symbolic importance and not merely the performance of mundane utilities' (p. 25). It represents the creation and policing of domestic order and concerns the detailed and intimate manipulation of time, space, objects and people. Homemaking and housework are then central to the reproduction of social order and arenas for the exercise of personal power. However, Hunt (1989) sees such personal power as more apparent than real. For her modern consumerism has not given women more choice in homemaking but harnessed them more fully in the relentless pursuit of domestic style.

Food practices are one element in the construction of this social order. Charles and Kerr (1988) describe how women's production of food and particularly 'proper meals' reproduce the patriarchal family and women's position within it. In British culture 'a proper meal' consists of a familiar meat-and-two-vegetables and involves the family sitting down to eat it. Hence 'Sunday "dinner", the proper meal *par excellence*, is also felt to be an important part of "proper" family life' (ibid, p. 227). Food practices are patriarchal in that husband preferences dominate the family diet, men consume high-status foods and the timing of the day's main meal must fit the husband's return from work. Hence women only produce 'proper meals' for other people and especially for men.

Food consumption is a measure of status and without a man to cook for there often seems less point in cooking. In the absence of a husband or partner, children become the basis of women's timetables. The timing of meals changes and they require less preparation and formality in their construction and consumption. Furthermore, many lone women do not eat 'meals' at all, but subsist on snacks and children's leftovers. Most husbands are routinely absent during the working day, and therefore non-residence introduces changes in the evening. Here women can be more flexible in what they do and they can operate a less strict timetable with the children as they have no need to make time for their husbands. The absence of a residential man alters mealtimes as pivotal points in the domestic day, and often leads to the abandonment of proper meals and the predominance of children's food in the family menu.

Graham (1987) adds another dimension, seeing food consumption by lone women and their families as an area of budgetary control. Food is one of the few areas where lone women in adverse economic circumstances can prune their expenditure, as housing and heating are largely fixed costs and areas where women can exercise few preferences. Graham details how lone women make simpler, cheaper, quicker meals using less meat. For some this reflects choice but for others it marks a deterioration of diet, sometimes for children and more often for themselves. The conclusions of this discussion can also be extended to elderly widows who so often lack the resources and the desire to 'cook'.

Although the home may be a small dominion in which women hold sway, issues of personal power surface in conflicts of gender and generation, as men feel managed by the homemaker and children feel impotent in the face of their all-powerful mothers. Women's efforts to organise the home, set standards and elicit their husbands' co-operation may lead them to be regarded as always nagging (Mansfield and Collard, 1988). At one extreme, retirement and redundancy may introduce or heighten marital conflict since they bring the husband's intrusion into the wife's domestic territory

(Mason, 1987; McKee and Bell, 1986); at the other, in households without resident men women gain a wider control and run their homes and rear their children more as they please. This analysis sees housework as more than economic labour – it is a cultural practice, and where women are without husbands the social rhythms of the household change.

In conventional families women undertake the lion's share of housework and childcare, and men, when they contribute, are primarily responsible for house maintenance and repair. Pahl's study of divisions of labour both within and beyond the household indicates the limitations of single-parent families: 'partners of different gender provide a convenient work unit . . . [Hence] single parent households are obliged to be more dependent on others; couples are more self-contained' (1984, p. 225). Couple-based households are more able to save money by self-provisioning. The average man may contribute little to 'housework', but those who are DIY enthusiasts can make significant contributions to the accumulation of housing capital by 'doing up' and 'trading up' in the housing market. Pahl found that single parents were more reliant on unpaid sources of informal help and that lone women often needed to 'borrow other people's husbands'. But the capacity of women to engage in such 'borrowing', even if meant in the most innocuous of ways, is limited. Women without husbands are viewed with reserve, if not suspicion, or are targeted by men with sexual ambitions. The very absence of a husband may then inhibit the inter-household exchange that Pahl regarded as so important to these families. As both self-provisioning and household exchange are difficult and the purchase of household services expensive, absence of men increases the skill of women in house maintenance as well as their self-sufficiency in decision making.

By contrast Weiss (1979) concluded that single parents did not run their households very differently from married parents, but that running it single-handedly was felt to be more burdensome. This is because the three main sets of tasks – income generation, housework and house-management, and childcare – all fall on one parent. For those in paid employment their days are punctuated by tight schedules, with weekends dedicated to housework and relaxation achieved only when children are in bed. However, the woman without a husband often has less housework to do. A resident man creates extra chores, more washing, higher standards for cooking, more organisation to suit his schedule, and women have to set time aside to be with him, to be attentive and accessible. Men's absence from the household implies a reduction in housework, as women are freed from some chores and freed from husbands' expectations, but it is not always experienced as a reduction, especially if the woman is not in paid employment. Husband absence alters women's interpretation of their days. Unpunctuated by his timetable, days become less structured and more featureless and single parents may feel more harried even when they have less to do. Also there is no possibility of sharing and no adult valuing of what women do. Even the idlest husband is a parent in reserve and 'a live-in substitute caretaker'. When absent there is no possibility of nagging or dragooning even a recalcitrant partner into helping.

These issues of domestic power and responsibility are also relevant in the study of husband-absent marriages. Gross (1987) discusses the domestic lives of couples who live apart, an arrangement which dislocates them in time and space, since they do not share a daily schedule or a single and common 'home'. Here career-committed individuals, and especially wives, could work with few interruptions, but the separations often left individuals feeling 'unmoored' and adrift from the anchor points that make daily trivia purposeful. There was also discomfort when relationships were renewed and ill-ease when visiting 'his' home and when 'they both have a "turf" alien to the other' (p. 221).

Temporary husband absence also increases the domestic power of wives, placing them in control of decision-making in the home, and where returning husbands do not or can not make such decisions and are sometimes ignorant of how everyday things in the house operated. The naval wives who were practised in husband absence described the inevitability and usually the ease with which they took over the house, making decisions and performing the tasks they thought in 'normal' circumstances should be undertaken with or by husbands (Chandler, 1987). It was linked to the logistics of his being away, for if decisions were to be made the wife was the only one available to make them. Choice did not enter into it. They had dealt single-handedly with sorting out insurances, mending household appliances, the court appearance of a child, major problems in the schooling and health of children, buying, selling and moving house. One conclusion is that women are more versatile than men. They can take over, where men without women employ housekeepers, and remarry more often and more quickly. However, the changes were not experienced as a simple reduction in daily tasks. Most women did not discuss this issue in terms of power and control but in the language of responsibility and duty. Some naval wives went so far as to see their husbands 'living the life of a single man' and themselves heading a 'financially secure one-parent family'. Many had a great sense of the totality and the loneliness of their responsibilities. While their husbands could escape, they could not, since they felt a greater duty to be always there.

Women without husbands have a great sense of their own self-sufficiency and independence. The growth of private house-ownership has increased the managerial aspects of housework. There is property upkeep and insurance, and dealing with banks and mortgage companies. Women with husbands away are faced with fewer household chores, but with modern property ownership they have more to manage. Also where absence is only temporary there is an element of answerability to returning husbands for decisions that may have been made and having to explain suggests the delegated nature of their power. Answerability also prompts friction and resentment of husbands who criticise and upset a wife's careful arrangement of the domestic apple-cart.

When marriages dissolve the changes in household routine are more total and final. Where husbands are temporarily absent the changes are more elastic and related to the type and the length of the separation. The patterns and context of husband absence in turn alter how it is experienced. The wives of men who are away in prison share the stigma of the punishment and suffer the gossip of neighbours. Women whose husbands are working away from home experience different rhythms of presence and absence, varying from being away for the working week, to weeks at a time and through to months. Here the length and pattern of absence is influential on household routines.

The study of naval wives (Chandler, 1987) contained a comparison of short and longer-term absence. Men who were away at sea were absent for at least weeks and more commonly months at a time, while those who were working in distant shore establishments would be away during the working week, returning to their wives and homes for a weekend marriage, a pattern referred to as 'weekending'. When asked to compare weekending with longer-term separations the overwhelming majority of women thought that planned longer-term separations were preferable to weekending and substantially better than unpredictable stints away from home. Some even felt that the longer- and shorter-term separations were not the same type of experience. Longer-term separations required greater responsibility on the part of women, but enabled them to establish their own routines and would be matched with a longer stay at home. However, during long spells away it was on Sundays that wives missed their husbands most, when everywhere was shut and everyone else was in a couple.

In the weekend marriages of naval wives the pattern of the relationship was similar to that outside service life, given the significance of the civilian weekend, but there were other problems and irritations for wives in this arrangement. Only a small minority of naval wives had become so inured to weekending that the comings and goings of husbands were not experienced as separations and reunions at all, and most saw it as a disturbing influence on their marriage. Changes in routine were short-run and the weekends became cluttered as women found they had more work to do in tending to their returning husband and his washing. Women tried to cram the weekends with shopping and do necessary odd jobs around the house. There was also the desire to keep the weekends free so they could 'be together' with their husbands, since his weekday absence made the weekends more of a special time. The weekends were thrown into sharp relief and became a time when women made extra efforts in a number of directions, where, although they were doing extra housework it was felt that this should not interfere with the time spent together. As one woman commented, 'You have to say to yourself . . . that your routine must go to pot when they come back . . . If the place gets into a tip it doesn't matter because you're only seeing him for a couple of days.' But the anticipation of the short time together could also induce tension, rows and frigidity. Disappointment was common.

Gross (1987) found similar domestic dynamics among married couples who live apart. She suggests that 'Because time together is so clearly bracketed off from "other time", this very distinctiveness makes their period together more vulnerable. They are cognizant of "spoiled time" together in ways, I suspect, co-resident couples are not' (p. 218). She notes that few couples enthuse about the advantages of husband absence and most speak guardedly about is compensations. This is to be expected, for to find value in separation would radically undermine marital and familial ideology. However, some lone wives felt that there was less time and desire to argue and less interference in the organisation of the home and the upbringing of children. Where romance in relationships requires some sexual tension and an element of being unrequited, forced absence made for a more romantic marriage. Where relationships were strained in the marriage, absence could always be blamed, as couples could fantasise that things between them would be so much better if only they could be together more permanently. For women who disliked their husbands it also meant that he was only at home for a short period and his presence could be tolerated for that length of time.

Other contextual factors relevant to the experience of husband absence are the length of their marriage and the employment status of women. Couples that have been married longer are able to accommodate to separations better than the newly-married. In relation to employment the messages are more mixed. The domestic routine and a wife's timetable can be more flexible to the intermittent presence and absence of a husband if she is not in paid employment. However, wives with careers may value the time without a husband as a period they can devote single-mindedly to work. Other ambiguities are encountered by women whose marriages have dissolved. They are impelled by economic necessity towards paid employment, but the absence of a partner for domestic back-up may make this more problematic.

Household finances

Patterns of domestic control also relate to the management of household finances. Land (1975; 1979) exposed the myth of the male breadwinner some time ago; only a fifth of women live in households where they are wholly dependent on the earning of a male breadwinner. The notion of breadwinning describes an attitude towards income and resources, implying both primary control and primary status within the household. Irrespective of their access to household income, women regard their money as 'housekeeping' and approach it with the attitude of economising, of managing it on behalf of everyone and not as their personal income. The absence of a husband gives women greater control over their resources, although the overall level of these resources may be reduced. They no longer have to negotiate for money from a recalcitrant partner, or hide their own, often meagre, income from his depredations. Their income becomes a more regular and known quantity and they often feel more secure, as although they have less money, they have more control of it.

In Pahl's (1980) typology of household resource management, lone wives are, by default, operating a 'whole wage system'. Pahl suggests that 'when money is short . . . managing the family's income should be seen as one of the chores of the household, rather than a significant source of power for the spouse' (p. 319). Pahl describes the wife's management of the 'whole wage' as burdensome when she is managing limited means. This is the experience of many lone women, but irrespective of the level of financial responsibility, house maintenance and management is a chore and a worry. Even 'breadwinning' wives (Stamp, 1985) were often more aware of their responsibilities than their power, their obligations rather than their choices. Discussions which only view the issues as those of power rather than responsibility give only a partial view. Women without husbands often have a crushing sense of solitary control where the absence of someone to share it with or take a decision for you is sorely felt.

Wylie (1986) describes how lone women survive by becoming 'androgynous', since 'It goes hand in hand with becoming the breadwinner, the head of the house, the decision-maker. As women develop their so-called "masculine" qualities of energy, independence, aggressiveness, they will need to repress the feminine' (p. 72). For both Wylie (1986) and Cashmore (1985) the end of a marriage can have liberating elements and offer fresh opportunities for women, but not all women are comfortable with these new choices, especially if the price of their freedom is their impoverishment. Smith (1986) describes these responsibilities for the wives of prisoners as the wife's sentence, as these women struggle to run their homes unaided. Also feelings of responsibility arc hcightcncd in a culture which contains so many harmonious images of family life. Women feel disadvantaged when they compare their present situation not to the reality of the past relationship, but to these images.

The issues of control of domestic resources have been related to women who are without a husband or partner. However, they are also relevant to women whose husbands are absent from home for occupational or custodial reasons. The vast majority of these women become responsible for bill-paying and house management. They have considerable control of the household purse, irrespective of the monetary arrangements and the organisation of the household accounts. In the study of navy wives (Chandler, 1987) half the women had joint accounts with their husbands, but there was considerable variety in how these joints accounts were used. For some the jointness was only nominal as they did not use the accounts or possess a cheque-book to them, while others divided the monies within the account for their individual use and yet more had sole use of the joint account. There were also instances of the husband's personal account being used as a *de facto* joint account – he had the cheque-book and she had the cash-card and his identification number. The allocative system of household money was hard to identify when money was handled through bank accounts, the use of which was so variable. And whatever people's intentions, jointness in financial dealings was hard to organise when so much time was spent apart.

However, the routes towards greater control for naval wives were problematic. Joint accounts required considerable planning and communication or a wide margin of disposable income if money problems were to be avoided, since the two parties were in effect living apart but drawing on the same account. Other women had a parallel personal account, preferring the certainty of what they regarded as their own money in their own account under their own absolute control. These women rarely handed back full control of the household purse to the returning husband and their control of the household budget/purse increased with length of marriage and the move to privately-owned housing.

Domestic power and incorporation

Separations between public and private life, between work and non-work, have in the past been central to analyses of the lives of women. Much of the substance of women's lives is a product of the intersection of these domains. The area is concerned with more than the issue of their participation in paid employment. It includes the ways in which the domestic labour of wives is connected to and structured by the employment of men. Using the concept of incorporation, Finch (1983) and Callan and Ardener (1984) have explored processes by which a husband's work 'both structures her life and elicits her contribution to it' (Finch, p. 2). There are two dimensions to incorporation. Wives are more or less hedged in by the amount and the accessibility of their husband's earnings and the locations and the routines of his work, and wives are also drawn in as hidden workers, as practical and moral supporters.

The model is clearest where the husband is continually present in the home, when home and work are coterminous, as in the case of the family business and the work of the clergy. However the model is also used to describe the opposite experience, where the working lives of men necessitate them being away from home. It describes how the domestic world is harnessed to the routines of even distant work, a husband's prolonged absence from home structures the workings of a household, and company definitions of the correct and desirable behaviour of distant wives are influential. In this way exclusion comes to be paradoxically linked with incorporation and wives remain married to the job by the very fact that he is not there. There is some ambivalence in the model. Many wives without husbands can be placed at the incorporated end of being structured or 'hedged in' by their husband's occupation as their household routines are moulded by his comings and goings. However, within this structuring by a husband's timetable there is an argument for some lessening of incorporation in the greater marital space that husband absence brings, affording wives more control over their time and enabling them to develop more kin- or neighbour-based support systems. Also Finch suggests that temporary absence may give women some personal latitude, but this is the freedom of absence rather than of help.

There is another ambiguous aspect to the concept of incorporation. The absence of husbands for occupational reasons sometimes entails the radical exclusion of women, as for instance in the military services where wives are symbolically set apart (Macmillan, 1984). Here women are constructed as the antitheses of men, warfare and aggression. Similarly, the shore-bound wives of naval personnel are utterly removed from the day-to-day working lives of their husbands. The wife's contribution is to manage the home and any attendant crisis without requiring his presence or, at times, any communication with him. On a commonsense level, their lives appear to exhibit qualities the very opposite of incorporation.

Another dimension is visible when both husband and wife are involved in a family business but the husband is away. The classic example of this is found in the fishing industry. Porter (1983) describes the sexual division of labour in a Newfoundland fishing town. Here there is a rigid division of labour along sexual lines, backed by hostile imagery of women where 'Women, if not witches, are certainly strangers and "jinkers" who pollute the fishing so that they might not set foot in the boat or go near the nets' (p. 92). This attitude and imagery is common where men work together and other examples are found among men who work in mines and on oil rigs.

However, in the case of the traditional fishing industry of Newfoundland and parts of Scotland (Thompson, *et al.*, 1983) women played a vital part. Where they were involved in processing and where they disposed of the fish or ran the croft, the very interpenetration of economic and domestic labour and the absence of men gave them considerable power. But their importance is not always acknowledged. Porter (1983) argues that accounts in the area have been biased by male anthropologists gathering data from male fishing crews and dominated by the processes of catching the fish. In these accounts women are marginal figures who work quietly in the background. Traditional fishermen's wives had considerable independence, as they controlled the processing sector and sometimes sold the produce. On a wider note, Porter argues that the traditional life of the fishing community was hard, where no one had any real power and family co-operation was a necessity and economic survival depended just as much on men as women. Hence the public vesting of authority in men could cut little sway within the house, since men were not just dependent on women for domestic servicing of their non-work needs but to process the fish and realise the value of the catch. This picture drawn by Porter is, however, a backwards look at the community, for the advent of the frozen-fish industry has removed the economic dependence of men on women and given women access to independent income in the fish processing factory. As the fishing industry changes so relationships between men and women are transformed, altering the impact and experience of husband absence.

Conclusion

Family life is constituted in the minutiae of domestic routines and the absence of a husband or partner limits its forms. Women without husbands may have more personal elbow-room and control over domestic resources, but although they have unchallenged domestic power, they also have to shoulder the burdens of domestic responsibility largely unaided. Hence the experience of being without a husband is often uncomfortable, because of unshared domestic responsibility and because without a man the daily round of women may lack purpose and meaning.

Temporary husband absence raises the possibility of escaping some of the patriarchal elements of marriage without falling into the poverty experienced by some single women and many lone mothers. However, the organisation of domestic resources may be problematic when daily lives are not shared and when domestic routines established in husband absence are only temporary.

8

Relationships with children

The conventional family is built around husband, wife and children and its relationships are essentially complex and triangular. The relationship between husband and wife is mediated by their relationship to children and the interaction between mother and child is influenced by their relationship with husband/father. The loss or loosening of marital ties affects children as well as partners and this chapter will explore the consequent transformation of family life and the divergence of interest between women, men and children.

Studies in this area have concentrated on the psychological consequences for children of not having two co-resident parents and stressed the developmental damage this inflicts. However, where the dissolution in question is that of divorce the treatment of children can be seen as the exercise of power by parents and the courts. Although an uncomfortable frame of reference it reflects the social position of children and illustrates the importance of family politics after marriage. This chapter draws on both social psychological and political modes of discourse.

The increase in the divorce rate and in the number of children born outside marriage has led to the growth of single-parent households. In the past, pregnancy was a prompt to marriage, but today it is less the case – in 1977, 25 per cent of women in Britain got married as a result of conception, compared with 12 per cent in 1987 (OPCS, 1989). With approximately a third of marriages ending in divorce within fifteen years and a quarter of all children being born to unwed parents, the familial context of childcare appears to be changing. Presently in Britain 16 per cent of all households with dependent children are headed by a lone parent, 90 per cent of whom are women. Glick (1979) estimates that by the year 1990 only 71 per cent of children under eighteen in the USA will be living with two parents and, of the remainder, 25 per cent will be living in single-parent households and 4 per cent in foster homes. Taking a longer view, the number of children who will experience lone parenting at some time is far greater. Hofferth (1985) in the USA has estimated that 46 per cent of white children and 89 per cent of black children will have lived at least temporarily in a single-parent household before they reach seventeen. In Britain six out of ten couples who divorce have children and in the flux of family relationships more than half will also have gained a step-parent before they are sixteen.

There has also been some change in the legal context of childcare and children's rights. In 1987 Britain abolished the concept of illegitimacy, blurring the line for children between marriage and non-marriage, extending the rights and obligations of men towards their children outside marriage. The courts are also currently redefining the relative duties and responsibilities of divorcing mothers and fathers and deciding what is in the 'best interests' of the child.

As the discussion of wives and husbands changes to that of mothers and fathers, the clear gendering of relationships remains, as men and women are seen as playing different roles in the lives of their children and, whether the family is 'intact' or not, children are the daily responsibility of women. The desire to bear and nurture children features large in constructions of the female psyche. However, children's special ties with women continue to be legitimated only within the context of normal family life and there is no social approval for mothers who choose to go it alone. The circumstances of children who live in conventional families is rarely problematised. Concern for children is greater and analyses of their behaviour more prolific when 'the family' appears to be disintegrating, although fathers in normal families may be uninvolved with or violent towards the children, and mothers in normal families may not always be loving and caring. As elsewhere there are inadequacies of comparing atypical family structures with mythic accounts of 'normal' family processes. Nevertheless, it has been the putative needs of children that has raised popular and professional alarm about the apparent growth of family instability.

A fresh appreciation of children's experience of family life outside conventional families is needed. The developmental consequences for children are important, but also their reactions are influential on relationships between their parents and the processes of lone parenting. They may be used as lines and means of

communication between parents and they influence the establishment of new relationships and the constitution of new families.
These changes dissolve the conventional household and family
triangles of resident mother, father and child, as children routinely
live in lone-parent households but may retain strong ties with
multi-parenting families. The boundaries of the family blur as
husbands/fathers may come and go and children travel between
different households and stay with different members of their
family. Here there is a differential experience of childhood to be
discussed and appreciated outside the context and beyond the
yardstick of conventional family life. Despite the current panic
about 'family life' there are some contrary voices: Franks (1988)
sees the dissolution and reconstitution of households and families as
offering creative potential and the possibility of wider supports for
the child; Farley and Allen (1987) note the creativity and flexibility
of the matrifocal black family in its struggle with racism, poverty
and migration.

This chapter is concerned with the reactions of children to marital
dissolution and father absence, the qualities of lone parenting and
relationships with resident and absent parents, and public policy
towards them. In marriage children are largely the private concern
of parents, but in dissolution this is less the case. Also the chapter
hopes to give some indication of what these changed relationships
look like from the child's point of view, an area dominated by adult
consideration and interpretation of their best interests. In marital
dissolution there are clearer divisions of interest between parents,
and between parents and children, and these are magnified and
made more visible by the lack of conventional aggregate forms.

Women and children

Familism has been well discussed in relationship to women, but its
logic applies equally to all children. Alanen (1988) argues that
modern childhood is constructed entirely within the bounds of
family relationships and has few reference points beyond this.
Childhood is a time of protected innocence and this is guaranteed by
good parents and normal families. Children are important in
drawing the couple into a proper family and because of the
emotional and material investment that is made in them. Even if

children are not seen as marital cement, they are an affirmation of proper family life. Children are social seed-corn symbolising progress and the future and this influences their social personalities. In modern sociology children are significant as preparatory adults. As Qvortrop pointedly comments, 'Children are not human "beings" in sociological literature, but only human "becomings"' (1985, p. 132). Alanen (1988) argues that they are only seen in the context of the family and in relation to the processes of socialisation. They are considered largely as objects of their parents' care and concern and parental efforts are judged in terms of their success in fitting the child into the community. In the context of marital dissolution or atypicality, the search has then been for signs of abnormality and developmental scarring and children are scrutinised and parents assessed for evidence of poorer socialisation. New family arrangements are evaluated against definitions of childhood and socialisation that have been developed within a 'particular *version* of "the family". It is little wonder that this often results in explicit or implicit moralism and pressure towards normative family policies – naturally in the interests of providing the best for our children' (Alanen, 1988, p. 55).

Smart argues that the familial dependence of children means that they 'are hardly recognised as legal persons', since their 'recourse to law is couched in terms of protection rather than rights, with the consequence that the state and parents have the right to do things with children "for their own good"' (1989, pp. 3–4). As with analyses of women, discussions of children are overwhelmed by assumptions about their place in normal family life. Where the structures of families do not fit this model, the language of the debate is that of deficiency and lack, not of difference.

Their relationship with children is a key aspect of the gendering of women. Custody of children is largely defined as a female preserve since children are seen to need their mothers and, where children are young and themselves female, the claims and responsibilities of women go more or less uncontested. Hence the debate on lone parenting is primarily concerned with lone mothers, as in divorce women are given custody of 85 to 90 per cent of children. They are seen as having clearer day-to-day responsibility for children and innate skills in the nuts-and-bolts of child rearing. Divorce and separation sharpen the domestic division of labour in relation to children which forms the basis of public policy – women are seen as concerned for their physical care and men for their economic maintenance. Lone fathers are judged as brave and self-sacrificial, as undertaking an unusual and difficult job, whereas the images of lone mothers are less generous.

As the concept of childhood is bounded by socialisation and familism, children are essentially seen as the recipients of social influences, passive in social processes and the object of good and bad parenting. In this frame children do not have the same ontological status as adults. They are not social actors and are never attributed with powers of social agency, as they are seen to play no part in the construction of their own social world. They are only co-operative or recalcitrant, whole or damaged, within the world of adults.

For Jenks (1982) the model of childhood was constituted to support a particular model of social order and adulthood and he argues for a programme to make children conceptually visible and active in social analysis. It is only when 'normal' families collapse or fail to be formed that there is a significant interest in children. Although feminism has instituted a strong programme to make women more visible, there is no similar programme for children. Within much feminist research children maintain a residual status, a form of social baggage, confirming the housewife's domestic identity through the duties and the emotional ties of motherhood. There is, however, great scope in feminist literature to examine the status of children and their relationship to women and the power structure of the family. Also although feminist research has taken a critical look at mothering, it has been less eager to examine the relationship between children and men, although this is so often the contested area in atypical families.

An examination of the relationships with children in 'normal' family circumstances also illuminates the nature of womanhood in our society. Past analyses have offered a unitary view of married women (Oakley, 1982), where the identities and tasks of wife and mother are entwined in the activities of 'housewife'. Such unitary assumptions ignore Bernard's older observation (1972) that sexuality and maternity are antagonistic in Western society and the further conclusion that motherhood and wifehood may be in conflict not harmony. In conventional families and companionate thinking, these elements may be deceptively rolled together but, where fathers are dead or absent, women become specialist mothers and do not have to divide themselves and their availability and loyalty between children and husband. In divorce the care and control of children becomes a matter of dispute and state intervention, and increasingly the courts are being called to arbitrate when cohabitation ends. Dissolution alters the organisation of the household, an issue which has been discussed in Chapter 7, and it alters women's relationships with children.

Reactions to loss and dissolution

The complexities of loss and dissolution make any assessment of their impact on children somewhat difficult. There are immediate reactions and long-term consequences, adjustment to parental absence and to the restructuring of the household and its routines. Also both death and divorce may not be sudden events – death may have been preceded by a long disabling illness and divorce may happen some time after a more stressful separation. The time-scale of the research and the lead-up to dissolution are relevant factors, as 'intact' families often do not suddenly and mysteriously fracture. There are the problems of sheer absence, the pain of simply missing someone, and the strains of becoming accustomed to changed domestic circumstances, to the realignment of relationships within and beyond the household. In the context of divorce there is also the possibility of continuing conflict between parents within which the child is frequently embroiled. Here any description of a child's behaviour is inseparable from its interpretation by family members and others. This can be seen in a number of related ways.

First, research programmes are designed to measure the developmental progress of children in these atypical families as against children in 'normal' families, to see if they fall short of their mark. The worst of these studies are undertaken without a control group and with groups of children derived from disturbed or delinquent populations. Second, there are the interpretations of families themselves as their sense of domestic incompleteness or failure leads them to scour their children's behaviour for signs of personal damage and to attribute failings, bad behaviour and their own difficulties with children to the 'brokenness' of the home. Single parenthood may only highlight common problems with parenting, but these problems are harder to explain away in the single-parent household.

Third, an interpretation of loss and dissolution is influenced by an often rosy view of the past. Our vision of the 'intact' family does not go back very far and largely derives from the Victorian middle classes. The early twentieth century was a time of demographic change, with rising life expectancy and the birth of fewer children into more narrowly defined child-bearing years. Here the family experiences of children may have been more stable than at any other historical time. The work of historical demographers has done much to uncover the actual impermanence of many marriages in the past. In the sixteenth and seventeenth centuries Laslett (1972) estimates that about a fifth of dependent children lost at least one parent by death and many more were born to unwed mothers or were the victims of desertion.

There are many similarities in children's reactions to death and to divorce. Both are accompanied by feelings of loss and stir a surfeit of raw emotion, feelings that unsurprisingly mirror those of adults. The reaction of children to death varies with their emotional and cognitive development. Young children who have not acquired an adult concept of death have been seen as incapable of mourning, but this then depends on the range of behaviour that is to be regarded as grieving. Burgoyne (1984) argues, in relation to divorce, that children are more prepared than adults suspect, in that they sense the family change. However this is not always the case, as many children do not suspect that anything is 'wrong', feeling that the family rows and atmospheres are normal, or if they are not 'normal', that they are not subject to change. Although friends' parents may have split up their own family structure appears immutable. The death of a parent may be equally beyond comprehension. In the structuring of the contemporary family a parent may be such an omnipresent figure that life without them is literally unimaginable.

Children's reactions include anger with the departing or dying parent, guilt in that they suspect the disruption to family life is their fault and regression to earlier patterns of behaviour, as normal childhood development is halted and routine ways of acting thrown into disarray. Amid this there is the overwhelming desire for the missing parent to remain or return and powerful fantasies about the re-establishment of family life. Children are hostile to change and conservative in their relations with parents. As the missing parent in the case of divorce or temporary absence is usually the father, children's reactions are complicated by how they are treated by their mothers, who themselves may be anxious and, in their own distress, less able to support their children. It is also common for mothers to become initially restrictive and authoritarian. But however they react, parenting does not continue in the same way as before. Amid the trauma and the loss, just like adults, children also have pragmatic concerns and are keen to know how the changes in domestic circumstances will impact on them.

However there are differences between death and divorce. The death of a parent is seen as wholly sad, as nobody's fault and it inevitably brings true lone parenting for the child involved. Divorce is always tinged with moral culpability and brings more guilt where there are children. Here the 'broken home' is contrasted with the 'intact family'. Public authorities are also more ready to intervene for the sake of the children, who are judged the only true innocent parties in the disruption of family relationships.

Although children are seen as a natural and inevitable consequence of marriage, a form of marital cement, they also bring tensions into marriage. Studies of marital satisfaction show its steady reduction during the child-bearing years, and under the influence of feminism research has tried to push aside the myths of motherhood and look more critically at women's attitudes and experiences. Boulton (1983) describes women's feelings and interpretations on becoming a mother. Here babies add meaning and a sense of fulfilment to women's lives, but they may also introduce tension between wives and husbands. This is especially so when women give up a well-paid and absorbing job to undertake full-time childcare with its daily round of menial tasks. Children reaffirm a traditional domestic division of labour and this can create, whatever the meaning of motherhood, a sense of relative deprivation for women in their marriages. Boulton found this was a particular issue among middle-class women, but its implications are wider. Children are not an unmixed blessing either in marriage or outside it.

Research on the reactions of children to divorce generally agree that what children want most is for their parents to be reunited, whatever the marital problems were (Wallerstein and Kelly, 1980; Mitchell, 1985). Failing this, they are anxious to know that the missing parent has not abandoned them and that the remaining parent will not also leave them. Wallerstein and Kelly found that over half the children felt their life stressed by family dissolution and only one in ten relief at the break-up of their parents' marriage and here relief was frequently associated with their own escape from the physical violence of an intact family. The misery of children may go unnoticed by the mothers struggling to reconstitute order and fresh stability in their own lives.

Wallerstein and Kelly argue that the ill-effects of divorce linger long and a quarter of the children in their study were anxious or depressed a year after the divorce. But again there is room here for false comparisons, as many children, especially in adolescence, are troubled and anxious and children themselves may use divorce as an explanation of their own misery. Children are sensitive to continuing ill-feeling between parents and, what disturbance to their behaviour there is, often relates more to present conflict than being a legacy from the past. The feelings of children are affected by poor communication and inadequate discussion or explanation of their new situation. Also the distress of children may not be manifest, as many hide and bottle their feelings, to prevent further hurt to the remaining or resident parent and, relatedly, they may conceal their desire for greater contact with the absent parent, as this appears disloyal.

In divorce the reactions of children revolve around the twin issues of absence and conflict, issues which Lund (1984) attempted to disentangle by comparing children of parents who had developed different relationships after divorce. There were parents who were co-operative, others who were in touch but antagonistic, and a third group where contact had been lost with the non-resident parent. Children in harmonious separations and divorces were reported by parents and teachers as better behaved and better adjusted, while those whose parents were more antagonistic were more angry and less well adjusted. However, those from absent-parent families were seen as having the greatest number of emotional problems and the lowest self-esteem.

The absent parent has been researched in a number of contexts which include those absent through marital dissolution and those away from home for a variety of more or less temporary reasons. Intermittent husband absence has been investigated in relation to possible disturbances amongst children and in this context one of the most popular research fields has been the service family. The behaviour of boys is viewed as especially problematic in the father-absent household and research suggests a tendency towards the over-dependence of children on their over-protective mothers. Women are seen as unable to compensate for the lack of a father and when they try this generates problems. Children of lone mothers appear to be over or under-parented – this is the 'catch twenty-two' of lone parenting. Again the research based on clinical populations 'demonstrates' the clearer connections between father absence and problems with boys. When controls are introduced there appear to be fewer systematic differences between service and civilian groups and variability within these groupings. It prompts questions about what is good lone parenting and most of the debate would have us believe that this is a contradiction in terms.

The behaviour and the distress of children can take on diverse and even contradictory shades of meaning in the conflicts between parents and the battles for custody. Parkinson (1987) gives a litany of examples: a child's refusal to visit the non-resident parent can be seen as evidence of the poor relationship the child has with that parent, as symptomatic of that parent's shortcomings or as evidence of the poisoning and indoctrinating influence of the other caretaking parent; an eagerness to visit may be seen to result from bribery and spoiling or from genuine love and attachment; a child's bad behaviour after visits may be blamed on their unhappiness during the visit or their maladjustment at home. In all these cases the remedy may waver between increasing or reducing the visits to the absent parent's home and, throughout, the picture is one of the child as innocent victim of the shortcomings of adults. Parkinson, however, also notes their contribution to troubled family relations, their involvement in familial adjustment, and their strategies to reunite divided families and torpedo the new relationship of their parents.

Throughout there is a sense in which children are plunged into problems not of their making, concern about how their misery is part of the changing relationships of adults, how they may be inhibited from expressing their own desires and interests, and how tactful they are in making allowances for the distress of adults. Also from the research the messages seem clear: children are seen and see themselves as rarely benefiting from the dissolution of marriage; parents locked in combat is judged better than parental absence and, however difficult it is, some sort of joint parenting is seen as better than lone parenting. This research has also guided policy as joint custody in court settlements is gaining favour, especially in the USA.

Women as lone parents

Many women find themselves either permanently or temporarily in the position of being a lone parent to their children. They may be women whose marriages have ended, those who have never married and those whose husbands are at the moment away from home. The quality of lone parenting is frequently assessed in terms of its equivalence to an ideal model of the 'normal' family. Using this yardstick any difference is seen as a deficit and lone parenting is seen as a poor substitute for 'proper parenting'. Others, more defensively, are keen to argue that lone parents can do just as good a job as couples. The more important analytic task is to recognise the qualitative differences in styles of parenting and the ideological grip of the nuclear family, without reproducing that ideology.

Lone mothers are specialist mothers, as children are typically the only other members of their household. In these households there are fewer divided loyalties and no immediate father to whom children can turn and with whom they share their mother. From the mother's viewpoint there is no second adult to support or contradict them. Weiss's account (1979) of experiences and attitudes in such households describes how father absence alters a mother's relationships with children. Children may become the woman's main or only source of personal meaning as they are all that is left of 'the family'. In this context women may become more fearful for their children's safety or feel that their children are owed emotional compensation for living in an incomplete family. Mothers may become preoccupied with what they feel are the children's special needs, becoming hyper-alert to their children's emotional states, searching children's moods for signs of pathology or, if they have left a marriage, justification of their own behaviour. Within this there may be ambiguity, as mothers feel they should be more available, that their children should, in the absence of a father, have more of them, while also feeling resentful that they have to give so much and that the children tie them to the home.

Children living only with their mother become more involved in her decision-making, more atuned to her feelings. Weiss argues that single parenthood may strengthen household boundaries, drawing mother and children into a tighter-knit group, especially if children are older. They spend more time together and there is an increased interchange in their relationship. As described such a grouping appears cosy and harmonious, but the tighter links and the greater intensity of interaction is also the breeding-ground for conflict and bouts of rage and remorse. Creating adult space in the home may be difficult for lone mothers, but many find it essential (Hardey, 1989). Weiss also argues that the power structure of the single-parent household is unlike that with two resident parents. Where there is a couple the children are less involved in the processes of family decision-making and the parents are always in control. Parents act in collusion or one may side with the children against the other, but the possibility of there being another parent with or against whom to act is ruled out in lone parenting. The 'echelon' structure of the two-parent household, where parents as a cadre control children, collapses in the one-parent household. Hence single-parent households appear more democratic and more permissive, as they are inevitably less hierarchical. However, Weiss contrasts the apparent permissiveness of the single-parent family with the indulgence of the couple, as parents here retain an ultimate authority and require no necessary contribution from the child in the household. The child in the single-parent household is expected to be more self-reliant and to be responsible for younger children, particularly if the mother is also in paid employment. As children in single-parent households are encouraged to become more self-sufficient and responsible, they then cannot be parented in an authoritarian manner. For the busy mother arguments may take too much energy and wherever possible it is easier to compromise. Where lone mothers do demand obedience and take a more punitive stance, children feel more resentful.

The absence of a parental 'echelon' permits the child–parent relationship to be modified and Weiss argues that it is only the most self-reliant mothers and rigid of single-parent families that do not change in this way. However, the changes are not without their problems: with older children the mother may feel displaced or dominated; with sons there is the possibility of recreating a relationship imitative of the husband–wife duo, and with only daughters the dangers of intense identification; in the struggle for mother's affection sibling rivalry increases. Discipline can also be a difficult area. As lone mothers become more emotionally and practically dependent on their children, they become enmeshed in negotiation and it becomes harder for women to make children toe their unsupported line, to retain firm and unquestioned standards.

Thus parental privilege is more likely to be questioned and parental space invaded.

The circumstances of lone parents are often given a gendered interpretation, which emphasises the weakness of lone mothers and the problems of controlling adolescent boys, and many women themselves see the problem as one of gender rather than the situation itself. They believe that it is because they are women that they cannot act authoritatively. Furthermore women may feel anxious about not being able to impart gendered knowledge to their sons, about shaving, about life in general (Burgoyne, 1984). They fear they are bringing up children within a more feminised household. These fears link to traditional definitions of masculinity and fatherhood. Aside from issues of control, Lasch (1977; 1979) has criticised feminised family life as not offering boys the developmental benefits of struggling against a patriarchal father.

Many of these issues also apply to women whose husbands are temporarily absent from home. Children become the basis of their timetables and home becomes less formal and more flexible, and in tune with their own and their mothers' wishes. For these women solo parenting may present fewer problems than the reintegration of husbands/fathers within the household, an issue to be more fully dicussed in the following chapter.

The most perjorative view of the single parent held about the unmarried mother. Here motherhood is seen as manifestly delinquent, as the product of unlicensed sexuality. Women are criticised for bearing a child they cannot economically support and for giving the child a bad start in life. In earlier years they were frequent inmates of the workhouse. In the latter part of the nineteenth century homes for unmarried mothers were established with the aim of rehabilitation, where a young woman could give birth to and be with her baby for a short period of time before the child was fostered out or adopted. The young woman would then be found a suitable place in domestic service (Spensky, 1989). Where grants for the child to remain in a nursery were available from such organisations as Dr Barnardo's, the grant was conditional on their continued respectability and 'good behaviour'. Also there have been historical variations in the extent to which the unmarried mother was seen as culpable and punishable, with women who had chosen to become unwed mothers seen as more reprehensible than those who had entered into motherhood more unwittingly. The debate continues as there is present anxiety about rising numbers of unmarried mothers and their claims to housing and welfare support. A recent study of young single mothers describes how most had drifted into motherhood (Clark, 1989), finding themselves pregnant but electing to keep the child. Any decisions that they had made were uninfluenced by housing or welfare eligibility and most, although experiencing problems of support and accommodation, wanted to consolidate their household and find suitable training or employment.

Children and the absent parent

In atypical family structures, children may regularly visit and be partly the responsibility of a parent who does not live with them. Familial rights and obligations are moved beyond the household to alter the relationship of the child to both the resident and the non-resident parent. Aside from differences of behaviour and interaction, parenting may be more self-conscious and the fissures between parents more obvious. As it is mothers who largely obtain custody, the absent parent is likely to be the father. Here the child's ability to sustain a relationship with an absent father is difficult and regular contacts tend to fade with time. Children move between households and here they encounter different standards and assumptions about behaviour in the home and become privy to information about the private life of the other parent. Children are often unruly and disturbed after visits to father, as these visits restir the child's emotions and the child is subject to different rules and disciplinary practices. Also, during the visits, the father may wish to compensate for the loss of residential parenting and give the child an abnormally 'good time'. There is also possible tension with their mothers, as children may want easy access to their fathers, but mothers do not want ex-partners intruding into their redefined private domain.

As children move between households they are used in the continuing relationship between parents. They may act as go-betweens, carrying messages between the estranged partners and learning tact and discretion. Parents may seek to manipulate their loyalties in their continuing battles or justification for their own behaviour. Parents may disguise their own desire to talk to the other partner in the language of concern over the children. As in all relationships children form with adults, they are relatively powerless, although not passive. They may exploit divisions or foment drama, often intended to reunite the estranged couple.

Frequent visits to an absent parent demand geographical proximity but when they occur they have an economic benefit. Men who sustain a relationship with their children are more likely to contribute to their economic maintenance. However, contact with the absent parent tends to decline over time and especially as the ex-partners establish new relationships. Troph (1984) gives a conservative estimate of the extent to which children's contact with an absent father is lost in the USA – 12 per cent of fathers lost contact with children after divorce, 23 per cent after their own remarriage and 31 per cent after the wife's remarriage. Mitchell (1985) found that over a quarter of children lost contact with the non-custodial parent on divorce and in N. Ireland the figure has been placed at half (McCoy and Nelson, 1983). For those non-residential parents who maintain contact the frequency of visiting tends to decline as the child gets older, but when they do visit this tends to be for a longer time. Even parents with good intentions find it hard to maintain a visiting pattern over time. Their own desire to start afresh, the demands of new relationships and the difficult behaviour of children militate against its normality and effectiveness. Where children appear difficult or upset there is likely to be a gradual withdrawal by fathers. Also in the division of responsibility, mothers who have physical care of the child are in a stronger position to interpret what is best for them and this may lead to the exclusion of the father. However it is not always a case of inexorable decline and, whatever the care and custody arrangements, some children may change residential households. The commonest example is the adolescent boy who moves to live with his father.

Seltzer (1989) describes how in the USA the fathers of children born outside marriage are less involved in their care and support than the fathers of children born inside marriage. Mothers who are unmarried feel they have the least claim on their children's fathers, whether for maintenance or for active parenting, and they are most grateful if some support is forthcoming. Unless coloured by violence, relationships with former partners are less tense, probably because the woman's claim to the child is uncontested and contact with the father poses no threat to her relationship with the child. There is less concern that the child's affections will be stolen – or, even, the child kidnapped. However, where cohabiting unmarried parents separate the state may also become involved in the organisation of access and maintenance. As it does so it increasingly employs rules concerned with the ending of marriage.

Like other aspects of husband absence and marital dissolution the problems of children are couched in the language of emotions and relationships, although many of these problems may derive from the financial pressures and the insecurities of lone parenting. Also the social psychology of marital dissolution, while important, is apolitical in its analyses. However, childcare and custody in the post-divorce family is a continuation of the power structures of the 'normal' family and a key issue in the politics of gender. The allocation of rights and responsibilities between mothers and fathers is central to the legal construction of gender and the interpretation of the best interests of the child has become the remit of a growing band of professionals.

The role of the state

The state has an interest in the maintenance and care of children outside conventional families. There are benefits for widows and single parents, the prioritising of nursery places and concern for the treatment of children when parents become divorced. The provision for children in separation is regarded as a private matter, unless parents are seeking a judicial separation or one of the couple challenges the *de facto* behaviour of the other. Where a couple are formally dissolving their marriage, the courts have an interest in checking the suitability of those arrangements. Parkinson sees the court as undertaking 'a difficult balancing exercise in trying to maintain the parents' autonomy while exercising their statutory duty to regard the welfare of the child as the first and paramount consideration' (1987, p. 72). As children are increasingly seen as the victims of their parents' divorce, the courts are developing separate services for child advocacy, reformulating parental rights and attempting to shape the workings of the post-divorce, and in some instances the post-cohabitation, family. In this way children's welfare legitimates the regulation of gender and the continuation of aspects of marriage.

The model of decision-making assumes consensus between the parents and research suggests that this may be superficial or non-existent. The very term 'custody' emphasises control rather than care and Parkinson also argues that the terminology and the procedure are, like all aspects of divorce, divisive and adversarial. While this may be appropriate for adults it is seen as harmful for children. The division of property and the care of children are the key points of tension in divorce and they are hard to distinguish, especially where custody of the children is coupled to the continued occupation of the matrimonial home. The Law Commission (1986) considers the problem of parental disputes to be minimal, as in only 6 per cent of divorce hearings is custody contested. But this low level of overt disagreement conceals a depth of dissatisfaction. Davis, MacLeod and Murch (1982) found that 29 per cent of parents were unhappy with the custody/access arrangements at the time of the divorce and 18 per cent had remained dissatisfied. In this it was men who were largely dissatisfied, feeling that the courts always favoured mothers. Judges have tended to regard women as the natural custodians of children, and this is only challenged when the child is presently living with the father, the mother is judged to be 'unfit' and where the child in question is a boy.

In Europe and America the presumption that women should have some natural claim to custody has been eroded in recent years by the greater introduction of joint custody arrangements. Its supporters draw on the body of knowledge that demonstrates that divorce damages chidlren and custody arrangements favour mothers. Joint custody is then seen as a legal solution to a number of divorce problems: it encourages a more companionate divorce which it is hoped will minimise child trauma; it appears to treat mothers and fathers more equally in stressing the continuation of co-parenting; and it satisfies the claims of men and more right-wing politicians that families need fathers.

However, the legal award of joint custody is commoner in the USA than in Britain, where in 1985 only 13 per cent of custody orders were joint. While joint custody is seen as a tool of damage limitation for the ills of divorce, Brophy (1989) has been more critical of how it is implemented and its potential impact on women. She argues that the 'demand for joint custody is in fact a demand for joint legal custody, as opposed to joint physical custody' (p. 218). Weitzman (1985) regards the change as merely one of labelling and many new arrangements resemble what used to be termed 'liberal visitation'. Here women retain day-to-day responsibility for children, but fathers have greater rights of access and stronger powers to veto their decisions. Among the optimists joint custody is seen as a means of lessening hostility in divorce by reminding parents of their continuing joint responsibilities and of leading men to continue contact and maintenance. But for Brophy these moves may continue the unsatisfactory power relations of marriage, reducing women's post-divorce autonomy but not their responsibilities. It is the clear reassertion of patriarchy in the post-divorce family, as the continuation of joint parenting is the continuation of aspects of marriage. Collins (1990) also notes the increasing use of the courts by unmarried fathers in their applications for access and custody, although they have been much less successful in their requests than married fathers.

While joint custody has wide support there is variability in its implementation. The courts and their officers in Britain are hostile towards arrangements that veer towards joint care. They consider them a source of continued dispute for the parents and confusion for the child and there is a strong desire to place the child firmly within the boundaries of a single household and inhibit regular moving between two. Although parents are given powers to act independently, when there are disputes the courts can arbitrate.

Another aspect of the changing rules of custody is the interpretation of the best interests of the child. Although judges associate 'best interests' with what parents have agreed, or the status quo in childcare arrangements, and occasionally with what the child wants, the interpretation of 'best interests' is increasingly the task of the professional of para-legal welfare workers whose decisions give the illusion of objectivity and impartiality. Fineman sees the rhetoric of the child as obscuring 'a struggle among professional groups, special interest groups (particularly fathers' rights advocates), and legal actors, over who controls both the substantive standards and the process and practice of child custody decision making' (1989, p. 36). For Thèry (1989) child advocacy is not the sensible rejection of inappropriate court contests, but a reduction in the powers of mothers to define what the best interests of their children are and the start of closer scrutiny of non-marital mothering. In this way child welfare becomes a stronger instrument for the regulation of women.

Aside from gender politics, the desire for joint parenting constantly conflicts with the efforts to construct new nuclear families. Whatever the aspirations of the courts, and the parents themselves, towards the continuing involvement of fathers, there are practical obstacles. The absence of rules about how new and ex-partners should behave and be treated, and the calls of fresh relationships, dampen jointness. Other public agencies are equally hostile. For instance schools prefer to deal with the one parent who is clearly in charge of the child.

Finally, the child is stigmatised by the public knowledge that they come from a 'broken home'. Because of this their behaviour may be examined for signs of distress and delinquency and where their behaviour is found wanting the 'broken home' then becomes the catch-all explanation. Such labelling is widespread and becomes more infectious as agencies, such as schools, seek to adopt what they regard as a more pastoral role. However, the labels do not always work to the disadvantage of the child. The welfare report on a young offender that uncovers a 'broken home' in the child's past can be used as a plea for clemency and understanding, a plea which the courts may regard sympathetically or interpret as a reason for greater intervention and firmer control. Whatever the outcome, such information is never neutral.

Conclusion

In discussions of familial instability, children are seen as the main victims of change and their interests are distinguished from those of their parents. Although they are seen as innocents in the events, children are active participants in the household and family structures that flow from them. The loss of a parent, by whatever means, traumatises children, and to loss are added the difficulties of getting used to new household rhythms and relationships. Most lone parents are women and some of the qualities and the experiences of lone mothering are unlike those found in two-parent households. Mothering is disconnected from and unshared with wifehood and there is no parental echelon to act against the wishes of the child. Mothers may be forced to negotiate more with their children and this gives the one-parent household the appearance of a more permissive family structure.

The courts have tried to develop procedures and post-divorce arrangements that minimise disturbance for the child and increasingly favour joint custody. The administration of father rights limits the autonomy of women but may lead to fathers being more willing to continue to financially support their children. But these policies appear to contradict moves to produce a sharper and financially cleaner end to marriage. Furthermore the firmer tying of men to children has implications for couples exiting from cohabitation as well as marriage.

This chapter has been concerned with the implication of absence and dissolution for the children and their relationships with parents. But for many children and their parents dissolution and absence is not a final state. Fresh partnerships and marriages are formed and husbands/fathers return. Family life is reconstituted and the behaviour of children is equally influenced by and has influence on these changes. It is to this that the book now turns.

9

Reconstituting marriages and partnerships

In the dynamics of marriage, some women move to its margins, while the relationships of others move closer to its conventional forms. On a continuum of marriage, women pass both ways. Like disintegration, the reconstitutions of 'normal' family life form typical experiences within a life-course and women enter into fresh partnerships and rekindle relationships with returning husbands. This is part of the biographical elasticity of marriage. But, just as marriage may be a matter of degree, so is the level and nature of its reconstitution, as 'blending' may not be a smooth or complete process. Also there is a tendency to approach the issue through charting changes in marital status, but this only gives us a partial view of the flux in domestic relationships. Couples may marry after long-term cohabitation and, aside from remarriage, women may enter more loosely constructed relationships. Also, within marriage, absent husbands may be reincorporated in the home and intimate relationships resumed. In discussions of reconstituting relationships, the bulk of the literature is about remarriage and, although many new partnerships do not lead to remarriage, this literature sets the issues for a wider debate.

The concept of reconstituting family life is a normative statement about households, in that it refers to the restoration of conventional family forms. The reconstitution of the family is, then, a testament to the powerful ideology of the nuclear family as its influence is brought to bear on families whose members have been redistributed between households. New partnerships bring fresh public identities and may mean the end of such things as state support. Although the changes are largely seen as normalising family life, new relationships, remarriages and returning husbands are also problematic. Despite the dominant image of the 'normal' family, these reconstituted families remain different. When a woman in a new relationship already has children and/or and ex-husband, it is harder to assume the 'clean slate' and there is the greater acknowledgement of intrinsic tensions. Within these structures the assumptions of marriage are often more apparent than in first-time and unseparated marriages. There are more self-conscious efforts and awareness of the contradictions of family life. There is no easy terminology and no rules about how earlier relationships can be integrated with newer ones. Like non-marriage and ex-marriage, remarriage is another variation on a single social theme.

Remarriage in the past

Remarriage and the blending of families was as common in the past as today. Schofield and Wrigley (1981) claim that in the sixteenth and seventeenth centuries between a quarter and a third of all marriages were remarriages. But, although the rates are similar to today, in the past they drew on the population of widows and widowers and the historic meaning of remarriage differed. Because of limited access to divorce, remarriage was an option only for the bereaved but cohabitation was widespread although largely unrecorded. Gillis (1985) estimates that in the eighteenth century a quarter to a third of 'marriages' were irregular unions and in the nineteenth century a fifth of the population may have lived in illicit relationships. In the past the interval between bereavement and remarriage was short, with nearly half the men and over a third of the women remarrying within the year. Rates of remarriage fluctuated, its incidence tied to the nature of the economy and the ethics of the church, and its rates mediated by the age and sex of the individual. These factors shaped the marriage market for the widowed in pre-industrial Europe.

In England marriage has long been associated with the establishment of an independent household, and when land and livings were scarce marriage was delayed. Marriage to a widow or widower circumvented economic stricture as the younger person in the partnership acquired access to a land-holding and the older secured reliable help. At the time when the economy and the household were so intertwined, the death of a partner was an economic as well as a personal disaster. The economic motives for marriage could produce a pattern known as a 'marriage fugue'

(Hanawalt, 1986). Here, where there was no vacant land a younger man would seek an older widow in marriage, working the land until she died, then marrying a younger woman, who in turn would look for a younger man when widowed. Such a marriage/remarriage patterns also had demographic consequences. Remarriage offered some demographic compensation for high mortality and late marriage and the widowed constituted a 'matrimonial reserve army'.

Sogner and Dupaquier conclude from this that 'remarriage may be regarded as the first line of defence, entered into in order to safeguard the continued existence of the surviving members of the household' (1981, pp. 3–4). Remarriage was a means by which individuals shored up and sustained the household. It ensured survival and continuity and it was not uncommon for children born in the second marriage to be named after the first partner, an event almost unthinkable in the context of modern re-marriage. Modern remarriages are backed by the notion of the clean break and the fresh start, where lingering commitment to the past and earlier relationships are seen as detrimental and even threatening.

High rates of remarriage characterised pre-industrial Europe. However, in the nineteenth century rates of remarriage fell to less than one in ten of all marriages, a fall which was particularly sharp for widows. There are a number of reasons for this. The lengthening of life expectancy had raised the age of the widowed population. As emergent industrialism and wage labour detached the economy from the household and opened up other avenues by which younger men could seek their fortune, the comfortable widow lost some of her economic attraction. Also rapid remarriage following bereavement was no longer seen as seemly or respectable for women. In the fashioning of the Victorian bourgeois family it was assumed that the married couple be of similar age or the man would be older than the woman.

As today, remarriage in the past was most frequent among the poorer sections of society, among the younger age groups, and for men, and here utilitarian explanations of the variable pattern of remarriage fall somewhat short. The death of a spouse plunged both men and women into hardship but widowers were much more likely to remarry. Although women could more easily undertake traditionally men's work than men undertake that of women, other factors and the wider economic position of women were also influential. A second explanation emphasises religious attitudes. The Christian Church was equivocal about marriage, whether first or subsequent, and was more disapproving of women remarrying than men. Aries (1981) links religious opposition to the general attitude of the church towards a life in the world and of the flesh. With time its early asceticism was compromised and extended as marriage itself became a vehicle for church discipline. However, although marriage was incorporated into the ambit of the Christian Church in Europe from the ninth century onwards, remarriage, especially for women, remained stigmatised. Remarriage was a denial of her chastity and constancy, qualities valued and extended to beyond her husband's death. The respectable widow was to wear sombre attire, engage in seemly behaviour and even to withdraw to a more religious life. But ecclesiastical distaste for remarriage did not prevent it, since 'We know that remarriage was both frequent and widespread, yet it was, or seems to have been, generally disapproved of' (ibid, p. 27). Remarriage was tolerated as an alternative to destitution but was not recommended for the pious or the chaste.

As in marriage, remarriage had different economic consequences for women than men. In remarriage her economic rights were once more subsumed within those of her husband. Remarriage then limited her economic independence and confused children's right to inherit. Hence women were both more stigmatised in remarriage and more equivocal about its benefits. These influences are related, as marriage to a widow brought access to assets and she was a good catch for the aspiring suitor. However, as industrialism proceeded, as capital grew and the financial manipulation of assets became more sophisticated, widows were distanced from the control of these assets by the trusts formed by their husbands keen to protect their property against the risks of their wife's remarriage. Remarriage also attracted the keen and often negative interest of local communities. Community opposition was common in Southern Europe, expressed in the tradition of *charivari*. This custom loosely translates as 'rough music' and was a ritualised and noisy protest made to the remarrying couple by the rest of the population. The popular hostility to remarriage also provides a theme for folkstories, moral tales about the jealously and cruelty of wicked step-mothers.

Contemporary remarriage

In the past the remarried population was dominated by widows, whereas today remarriage is overwhelmingly the province of the divorced. The coupling of remarriage to divorce colours the debate. However, this of course does not mean that there are fewer widows, but that most are substantially older than divorcees. Age reduces their marriageability, and without dependent children the imputed economic need for remarriage is less pressing.

Although there are strong parallels between the experiences of remarrying widows and divorcees, there are also important difference. Images of the remarrying divorcee are more critical and their predicament and behaviour is linked to volition rather than force of circumstance. The pattern of divorce and remarriage has been termed serial monogamy or sequential polygamy, concepts which themselves contain more than a hint of criticism. Both underline the contradiction between the facts of widespread marital dissolution and subsequent formation of fresh alliances and a view of marriage as life-long commitment. But despite the instability of the married population, marriage is not seen as a provisional relationship. For Furstenberg and Spanier (1984), the pattern of conjugal succession is one that recycles the family. This emphasises the impermanence of both marriage and divorce but subverts the chronology of biography. Recycling assumes that individuals can return to the beginning, that they can start again, whereas biography is located in and bound by linear time and maturational forces. For the individual, patterns are not cyclical and new partnerships and remarriage are rarely unencumbered fresh starts.

A return to a world of being single is for women not like a return to one's younger years. The establishment of new relationships with men is often difficult for maturer single women, as has been said in Chapter 4. There are the problems of singles-bars and heterosexual meeting places are often geared to the younger age groups in society. Friends may make introductions, but this can lead to awkwardness if the person introduced is 'unsuitable' or the nature of the introduction creates moral pressure for the relationship to be successful. Mixed clubs and societies may be routes to meeting potential new partners, but they are largely used by the joining middle classes. Most of the new relationships formed by the single parents in Weiss's (1979) study had developed 'for want of anything better'. They were often seen as an emotional stop-gap, where there is less commitment, only tentative planning and caution as a 'visiting' relationship moves towards cohabitation. Many enjoyed the more relaxed relationship where they felt there was 'someone in their lives, but not cluttering up their homes' (ibid, p. 230). Although for some this was a stage in the slow move towards remarriage, for others remarriage was regarded, at the time of the interview, as a retrogressive step. The recycling of the family denies the march of time, the important differences between first and subsequent marriages, and it is not inevitable, as women enter long-term cohabiting relations and may elect not to remarry at all. Hardey (1989) found that many lone mothers were reticent about forming new relationships, and especially marriage, instead preferring more tenuous non-residential relationships with men. As cohabitation becomes a more favoured relationship among the divorced, rates of remarriage decline and personal relationships become more variable.

Remarriages now account for a third of all marriages that are formed, a figure comparable with that for pre-industrial Europe. As in the past men remarry more often and more frequently than women and the propensity of women to remarry is mediated by age. Over two-thirds of divorced women remarry but while the chances of those under thirty remarrying are similar to those of the single population, the figure falls to 56 per cent for those in their thirties and to 28 per cent of those in their forties. Statistically, these remarriages appear more unstable than first marriages: controlling for age, a divorced woman's remarriage is twice as likely to end in divorce as her first marriage and a man's remarriage is one and a half times more likely to end in divorce. Consequently, the dissolution of remarriages now makes up almost a quarter of all divorces.

In remarriage the age gap between partners is often greater than in first marriages. In first marriages 90 per cent of men marry someone younger than themselves compared with 10 per cent of women – the pattern is clear with an average two-year age gap between men and women. The picture is more variable in relation to second marriages, where 75 per cent of men remarry women younger than themselves compared with 37 per cent of women marrying younger men. In addition, the age gaps can be substantially larger than in first marriages. This may be because the age rules and courtship patterns of the young appear to lose some of their force when applied to an older population.

Class is also influential. Analyses of divorce in terms of the husband's socio-economic position show an inverse relationship – the divorce rate rises with the fall in socio-economic status. However, if the independent earning capacities of men and women are used and women's income is not aggregated to their husbands, the propensity to divorce adopts a different pattern. At the lower end of the scale divorce remains associated with material deprivation, but rates are also high for well-educated and salaried women, a level at which divorce rates decrease for men. Furthermore, women in well-paid jobs are also the least likely to remarry as these are the women in command of adequate resources to remain unmarried and the least comfortable with traditional male dominance. This is the group of women most able to resist remarriage.

Remarriage adds new refrains to the theme of marriage and a new context within which to apply the rules of conventional family life. It influences relations with spouse, wider kin and children and, as it creates blended families, these show continuities with and divergence from what is thought to be normal family life. There are also questions about how post-divorce cohabitation is like remarriage and how blended are the family relationships formed in this mould.

Blended families

A strong theme in the discussion of remarriage which emerged in the work of Burgoyne and Clark was the role of remarriage in the restoration of normal family life and the provision of a wholesome environment within which to care for children. For the couple themselves it was connected to a material happiness, to family treats and cosier homes, where the economic justifications for marriage are wrapped in the language of domestic security. Where there are children already, marriage is less obviously tied to the start of a procreative career, although there is a common desire to have a child of that particular union, to cement the relationship and to add authenticity to the family unit. This marks the desire to tie family and household more closely together and the urge to blot out the past and compensate for earlier failures and mistakes in relationships.

As couples in Burgoyne and Clark's survey (1984) 'made a go' of their remarriages their statements were in constant dialogue with, and sometimes generated additional tensions within, the blended family. Many of the problems and points of tension related to children in and beyond the household. Remarriage may finally end any lingering fantasies that children have for the reunion of their biological parents or fuel them with fresh anxieties. Children often do not blend and may refuse to be co-operative within a reformulated family. They may devote much of their energy to undermining new relationships and may act very divisively within their new household/family structures. As Franks (1988) points out, in the classic folktale Cinderella is utterly blameless, a victim of vile treatment meted out by a wicked step-mother. Real children often play a more active part in conflict with their parents' new partners. Also it should not be forgotten that biological parents can be equally 'wicked' and relationships with 'real' mothers and fathers equally stormy.

However, the notions of ill-treatment of step-children fit the assumptions and language of the nuclear family, with its valuing of intense parenting. Here children are seen as either inside or outside families, where they must be either included and step-parents engage in full social parenting, or excluded and pushed to one side as the newly formed couple become intensely preoccupied with one another. The age of the child is relevant to how far step-families can mimic the conventional, as step-fathers are much more likely to become social fathers to children under the age of five. With younger children it is easier to sustain their public presentation as a 'normal' family and relations are less stressed than those with maturer children.

Burgoyne and Clark (1984) asked partners in reconstituted households about how they dealt with nakedness and the intimate care of step-children. This was used to gauge the degree of closeness between step-parents and children. Despite great variability in attitudes between households, it was indicative of the extent to which partners also became parents, although recent heightened awareness of the sexual abuse of children problematises issues of intimacy within the family and its relationship with step-parenting.

Linked to the issue of normalising family life were the

interpretations parents placed upon their situation. Entry into a second marriage is often undertaken with more caution and there is a greater desire to make it work. Hence present problems whose airing may threaten the new marriage were ignored or more often redefined as legacies from the past or as temporary hiccups. Burgoyne and Clark (1984) saw this commitment as more important than the actual pattern, as 'Some . . . used their past experiences of each being single parents to develop new patterns of responsibility, others returned thankfully to a more traditional division of labour' (p. 163). In the language of the remarried the happiness of the couple was reflected in their interpretation of the security and well-being of the children. What people said they did was infused with models of good parenting, even when the parenting relationships were less than straightforward. The remarried have a strong urge to normalise, but Mitchell (1985) found that children were more hostile to new partners than parents had indicated.

However, substitute parenting brings other problems in its wake. Discipline and the legitimacy of control of children within the household are sensitive areas. Blended families often blend different standards and daily understandings of normal behaviour. They are more prone to factions, tugs of loyalty and the blaming of the absent parent for the child's faults or misbehaviour. Family ties beyond the household interfere with and invade the privacy of the new family and provide a scapegoat for difficulties with children, who in turn may be blamed for tensions between the remarried couple.

In the experience of remarriage, gender is important. Ihinger-Tallman and Pasley (1987) summarise main findings in the area stating that 'boys have an easier time than girls, and children in step-father families have an easier time than children in step-mother families'. Step-fathers may be seen as taking the mother away, as an intruder in the home and as a poor substitute for a biological father, a figure often romanticised by his absence. Step-mothers may face more severe dilemmas, expected to wash children's socks and cook their meals, but denied the disciplinary edge of a 'real' mother. The quality of step-relationships also relates to the extent to which children are seen as obstacles to the early intimacy of the newly formed couple and the wider nature of mothering and fathering. Step-mothers may feel impelled to 'mother' and this often provokes hostility and resentment. The guides to the remarried are clear on this issue. Whatever the urge to rescue and reform the children brought into the new partnership, step-parents should resist it and assume that they will not be the object of their partner's children's affection (Franks, 1988). The assumption that step-parents are substitute parents tends to generate hostility if not rebellion. The isue is particularly relevant for the partner of the custodial parent, and because of custody arrangements this is usually the step-father.

Names and terminology create difficulty, especially in public situations: the use of the terms 'mum' and 'dad' for step-parents may cause acute discomfort; the use of first names may appear to lack respect; the use of other kinship terminology, such as uncle, has an obvious phoney ring. Women may have to linguistically distinguish between their husband and their children's father. The existence of different surnames within the household may raise eyebrows and call for oft-repeated explanations. One solution to the ambiguity is for children to be adopted by step-fathers, although such a move is radically opposed to the assumptions of joint custody and is done at the expense of former fathers. But it draws the blended family into the nuclear fold, solving many household ambiguities, reuniting daily care more clearly with legal responsibility. There is often a partial transfer of responsibililty with the marriage of the mother as she may trade the end of maintenance for the cessation of regular visiting. In this scenario adoption is also a way of extinguishing the past. The dilemmas stirred by these trends may be magnified in a contemporary climate that calls for a more active and participatory fatherhood and the urges of concerned and responsible fathers may clash with step-fathers' impusles to nurture. The new family may cohere around the negative evaluation of the former spouse and the negative traits of children may be traced and projected onto other non-resident family members.

Remarriage also colours family events and decision-making. It influences when, and if, to have children of their own and how many to have, holiday arrangements, as well as behaviour at weddings and funerals. Second weddings are more subdued events, without the emphasis on either virginity or fertility and there are fewer assumptions about women being at the start of a procreative/sexual career. The ceremony is more likely to take a civil form as only 14 per cent of men and 10 per cent of women remarry with a religious ceremony – the discrepancy between the two figures occurs because more men marry spinsters than women marry bachelors second time around. Remarried couples cannot behave in the nest-building ways of other younger couples. Family decision-making may be complicated by age differentials, especially in relation to child-bearing and when other aspects of the life-course are poorly synchronised. Also late and subsequent marriage is a more pragmatic affair. Furstenberg and Spanier (1984) found partners were selected for their mutual interests and less because of their sexual attractiveness in relationships that were more overtly companionate.

Remarriages however have a high failure rate. Individuals may be marital recidivists, not learning from the problems of their first marriage or being more sensitive to, and intolerant of, the normal problems of married life. Remarriage is more likely to connect individuals who are at different points in their life-courses and this can strain relationships. The ambiguity of remarriage and the difficulties of blending families create the potential for rifts between the parties and undercurrents of stress in the relationships.

Remarriage also marks a return to a more private relationship as the couple become more self-sufficient and women look less to relatives for support. It is also a time when the state withdraws its benefits and contingent supervision. Problems over the state support of women may emerge when the relationship is that of visiting or cohabiting, as officials may asume it to be *de facto* marriage, with all its financial obligations. But, whatever the problems, a new partnership is socially interpreted as the end of an anomaly.

The desire to cement the new relationship may demand some pushing aside of a previously wholehearted commitment to children. Women can no longer specialise in motherhood and there is a clearer balancing of child and adult interests. As most custodial parents are women, children are more likely to live with a step-father. Hence women are at the centre of the household and act as the arbiters between their children and the new man. It exaggerates their role as family diplomats as they take on the difficult job of family integration. In addition to conflicts of loyalties there are clashes of financial interest in the redistribution of property and the transfer of income between households in the continued support of children, if no longer women. The economic responsibilities of former and present husbands provoke resent-ment as money paid in child-maintenance may be seen to benefit a woman's new partner, while the new partner may think the amount paid for child support paltry and resent having to subsidise the care of some other man's child. Also there is jealously and fear of lingering attachment to a former spouse where ties are not entirely severed.

Cherlin (1978) argued that remarriage was an incomplete institution because of the absence of clear rules about how estranged parents relate to each other and their children. He misidentified the problem. There are rules, but they are rules of nuclearity with its close connection between family and household. It is the application of these rules that creates the problem. The normative pressures encourage members to behave as if they were not living in a step-family, but a conventional one, and to limit wider familial responsibility.

However, all the discussion so far assumes that the trend is inexorably towards the emotional blending of step-families. The Caribbean culture provides a counter-example. Smith (1988), commenting on the rules of family relationships among consensual unions in the West Indies, notes the peripheral involvement of men in households. Men may form more than one consensual union, and contribute to the maintenance and schooling costs of children in different households. Smith also found little mutuality in many consensual unions, with women referring to their ostensible partners as their children's father and often being unaware of their partners' wider kin.

In white society in the West, cohabitation is more clearly associated with being a couple. Hence much of what has been written about blending families may equally apply to the co-habiting couple, although there are some differences. Even where cohabitation mimics marriage there is less pressure for families to blend, with less legitimacy for social parenting by new partners and no expectation that they will be received as mothers and fathers. This may limit the tensions of step-parenting by not moving towards conventional marital forms, or heighten them in providing no connection between a woman's children and her partner.

For a step-father to enter a family which for some time has been organised around mother and children poses some difficulties and these relationships may appear impenetrable. The research on reconstituted families emphasises their *active* making of family life.

Further examples of these processes are found where men are more peripherally involved in the household and where they are returning from long absence.

Returning husbands

Remarriage is often seen as part of a cycle, but this cyclical model is also popular when discussing husbands returning to their families. The return of a husband is a return to normality, the taking up of a relationship from where it was left off, and is evoked in the feeling of coming home. Schuetz (1945), prompted by the domestic implications of war, turned his perceptive eye to the intimate meanings that suffuse this notion of coming home. In absence the home forms a powerful symbol system, constructed out of all that is familiar and personal. Home is a synonym for the taken-for-granted and to return home is to stand outside social time, to re-enter an unchanged world and re-establish the familiar. However, social time does not stand still. Home is often not as remembered, as home has itself changed and its image has been elaborated and distorted in memory. Also people are not as they remembered. The notion of returning home is then self-contradictory, since 'the home to which he returns is by no means the home he left or the home which he recalled and longed for during his absence. And for the same reason, the homecomer is not the same man who left. He is neither the same for himself nor for those who await his return' (1945, p. 375).

In his comments, Schuetz is noting the effort that is required to reconstitute routines and the recurrent relations with the people and the things that make for home. He is suggesting that separations, even when they are recurrent, are never cyclical. The absent husband can never return to how things were. The home, the homemaker and the homecomer are inevitably changed by social events and the passage of historical time. These problems attach to all homecomings, but are most obvious in the context of recent marriage and the rapid changes of growing children. Apart from the more philosophical issues of never being able to return, homecoming husbands pose other problems. The discipline of the children, the increased capabilities of wives and ambiguity about control in the household can make his re-entry difficult.

The returning father alters the emotional structure of the family and provides scope for new emotional alliances. In naval families, some husbands found themselves competing with their children for a wife's attention and time, and wives complained that children did not want to surrender the exclusivity of their mother's interest (Chandler, 1987). By contrast, other women found themselves pushed to one side and ignored in their children's adoration of their father. Issues of discipline were a common and varied problem as there were changes in the pattern of parental control. Some children experienced its relaxation, as fathers re-entered the family by being lenient, by seeing their time at home as 'time out', a suspension of normal routines. In the eyes of their wives these fathers re-entered by spoiling the children and here wives felt they had more control over children when husbands were not there.

However, more commonly children were reported as apprehensive about the return of the family disciplinarian. There was tension about what the household rules were and who should impose them. Fathers who saw themselves as reasserting their place within the home, as taking their children more firmly in hand and as providing a necessary counterweight to their wife's leniency while away, were often resented by children and by wives. Women resented men's lack of understanding and over-correction of their children and often intervened to defend them. Others tried to understand the difficulties of their husbands. These men were seen as wanting to be like 'proper' fathers, but were often ignorant of the current quirks and foibles of their children, and unskilled in knowing when to intervene and when to turn a blind eye. This is a problem within all parenting, but routine or prolonged absence from home provides an ideal climate for misunderstanding and antagonism, where parents could have divergent expectations of children and where a sense of usurped authority can flourish.

Their children's reactions were interpreted and allowed for by wives in their relationships with homecoming husbands. Children were seen to be more naughty or more clinging to their mothers at these times. Enthusiastic fathers who overwhelmed their children on their return could be given a frightened reception if the children were young, and a frosty greeting if they were older. Other children looked forward to the return of father for the presents this would entail. Throughout, child reactions mediated husband and wife reunions.

Women left to manage households on their own frequently develop a strong self-suffciency and become accustomed to having everything in the home the way they want it. They become self-reliant and fall out of the habit of daily compromise. Left to their own devices wives learn the stance of fierce independence and personal capability and the hard lessons of coping on their own cannot be unlearnt on the return of a husband. Women who enjoy their own company, relish organising their own time, managing their house and their children without reference to others are those who 'cope' best with husband absence. However, these qualities, forged in separation, do not easily jell with the qualities of wifeliness anticipated by husbands on their return. A returning husband is faced with the matrifocality of his home, in which he may feel marginal, and an increasingly independent wife, whom he may find emasculating. Many of the more practised wives admit duplicity in feigning helplessness when their husbands were at home, in an effort to defuse and minimise tension in this area. The capability of wives may present a problem to a husband and some wives view the change within themselves with mixed feelings. While recognising its survival value, some see it as a hardening and 'unnatural' process.

Returning husbands also alter patterns of support and friendship amongst women. Even if strong links are established with friends while their husbands are away, on his return these intense relations are instantly dropped. On a naval estate, most women acknowledge the tacit rule of married quarters that women with returning husbands should be left alone for a time. Friends would respect the renewed 'privacy' of the home and women would see the domestic presence of their friends at this time as an invasion. Those more determined to hang on to their women friends would now pop in for coffee and a quick chat or meet at the shops, but shared meals and long afternoon outings were out. This was the pattern when husbands were away and at home for longer spells of time. When the 'cycle' shortens, as when men are absent for the working week and return only at weekends, this time becomes coloured by the meanings of reunion. The weekend is seen primarily as a time to stay at home, because of childcare problems and lack of inclination, especially on the part of the husband. After a hectic week husbands want to relax quietly and enjoy the novelty of being at home. Given that many women only had an evening social life when their husbands were home, this meant that they had almost no social life at all.

Conclusion

Women without husbands form a significant but ever-changing sector of the population. Many women who have become more marginal to marriage, especially those under forty, will later form fresh partnerships and some will remarry. These women will again find their lives shaped by the assumptions of conventional families. A strong theme of the process is the pressure to regroup familistic relationships within the contours of the household and to erode wider links. Other features of these relationships are their greater pragmatism and the ambiguities that they create when these subsequent partnerships overlay existent family networks. These partnerships rarely have the cleaner familial slate of first marriages and reconstitution does not always imitate conventional forms. Issues of reconstitution not only apply to new partnerships, but also to the reunion of wives with their temporarily absent husbands. As these men re-enter their homes, the lives of women are changed.

Where there are children remarriage leads to blended families, where new routines are hammered out and new households more or less accommodated to old families. A returning husband/father not only re-establishes relationships with his wife, he also has to be reintegrated into the relations and routines of the home. Lines of authority and areas of autonomy may be challenged or changed and the dyadic relationships with children shift into more triadic forms. The blend may not be smooth and the reintegration may not be complete.

10

Conclusion

Concern about marital breakdown and the dislocation of the family is once more preoccupying policy-makers and public alike as the final decade of the century arrives. This poses a number of problems to those interested in the changing forms of family life. Conventional marriage remains popular and has until recently been the focus of most sociological research on the family. The many women who find themselves in partial marriages or no longer married at all are treated as outside or only peripherally related to the debates on marriage. However, an analysis of these states and relationships is vital to our understanding of contemporary family life, as they are an intrinsic and regular part of it. Within the widened debate, the analysis of women without husbands has a double purpose that is difficult to simultaneously encompass. It posits quasi-marriage and non-marriage as distinct domestic and sexual states, alternatives to marriage. But it also sees these states as reflecting the nature of marriage and its connections to wider social structure.

Family life appears to be changing, but there are a number of problems in assessing change. The first problem is that it is easy to be blinded by the idealisation of the nuclear family. Firstly it influences our perceptions of the past. Post-war sociology often supported mythic accounts of the stability and extended nature of families in history. As historical demographers have more recently provided detailed pictures of households and families in former times, the extent of partial marriage and marital flux has become more apparent. The second difficulty is that it makes the area rife with false comparisons, as the lives of women are judged against a popular construction of the happy marriage. The idealised marriage appears in many guises, from the assessment of loss and dissolution to the search for a husband-equivalent in support. Hence the base lines for comparison are rooted in a companionate interpretation of

167

marriage and assumptions about the fundamental inadequacy of the lives of women outside normal marriage.

It could be argued that feminist research has balanced the debate by challenging these cosy accounts of marital symmetry. In the past twenty years it has charted the real lives of many married women and these portraits have often been stark and disturbing, but again these do more than reveal the 'truth' about marriage. They contribute to fresh constructions of its nature as these accounts are also interpretations of marriage and of gender. Women without husbands interpret their experiences in a number of ways and are often equivocal about the benefits and penalties of their situation. Consequently traditional accounts of marriage may diminish the advantages for women of life outside normal marriage and more critical accounts of marriage may overestimate how liberating the end of a bad marriage can be. Interpretations of marriage are all-pervasive, central to theoretical constructions of marriage and alive in women's own interpretation of their circumstances. This means that women compare themselves and their circumstances to what they feel happy wives and good marriages are. Here the urge to be part of a 'proper' and 'normal' family may be seen as the cure-all for troubles, while other women may be more reluctant to encourage any relationship leading towards marriage.

The changes in marriage are often interpreted as symptoms of its decline. As with all discussions of social trends it is hard to tease out what have been the substantive changes from the interpretations of the past and the present. One problem has been the analytic emphasis on marriage as a status rather than a relationship which gives a false fixity to its form. However, an analysis sensitive to the elasticity of marriage moves the debate to issues beyond those of breakdown and decay to ones which question the qualities of marriage, partial marriage, and non-marriage.

The issues of change and decay are also influenced by changes in the political climate. Here the right-wing trend in politics has been influential in a number of ways. The growth in cohabitation may mark a resistance to marriage, an extension of the individualism of the Thatcher years. Its growth is helped by the removal of the disabilities of illegitimacy and a legal approach that views it as quasi-marriage. Franks (1988) argues that families are back in favour, but that they have lost much of the potency and authority they had at the beginning of the century. However much families and marriage may be elevated as symbols of community and stability, they are undermined by other processes.

In economic terms the trend has been unerringly towards the liberalisation of the economy, where freedom for the individual translates into assumptions of economic individualism, and individualism for women challenges a patriarchal vision of the family. At a time when the talk is of demographic troughs the reserve army of female labour is again in demand, and in mature industrialism women workers are recruited to the growing number of temporary and part-time jobs in the service sector. Such trends undermine the traditional organisation of the family and hence the cries to bring back Victorian values seem feeble and the rumours of an impending Ministry of the Family appear bizarre. Although the symbol system of 'the family' does not sit comfortably with economic individualism, the greater effort to force men to support their children, if not their ex-wives and ex-partners, does. This policy grounds welfare provision in individual responsibility and gives individual responsibility a patriarchal form.

A discussion of the circumstances of women without husbands is a good vantage point from which to discuss conventional marriage. The dimensions of patriarchy and companionacy are entwined in marriage and both assume close connections between the power of men and domestic intimacy with men. The question then emerges of how relevant are these aspects of modern marriage for the women on its margins. Modern marriage puts a high price on friendship in marriage and commitment to the relationship, but the emphasis on emotion disguises the structural reference points of marriage. The emphasis on marriage as a relationship *par excellence* also works as much to undermine marriage as to support it. The importance of companionship in marriage has fuelled dissatisfaction with marriage, and if those petitioning for divorce are indicative it is women who are most dissatisfied. As the valuing of companionship has grown, more are leaving marriage. Another consequence of the growing importance of friendship in marriage is that relationships outside marriage become thinner and less satisfactory. It renders wives more dependent on their husbands, drains meaning from the lives of women without husbands and fuels the desire of many lone women for a new relationship, if not for marriage.

The relationship of patriarchy to the circumstances of women without husbands is no less complex. They have a measure of personal freedom that conventionally married women lack. They are not beholden to the patriarch within the home, but this does not mean that they have escaped patriarchy in any fuller societal sense. The restrictions on women with children may not even give them this measure of autonomy as the implementation of joint custody in effect gives supervisory powers to ex-husbands. Their lives are still bound by patriarchal influences of familism, which are built about assumptions of conventional marriage. Hence they encounter housing problems, experience poverty and are the objects of pity or scorn. They can participate in a subordinated labour market and/or seek relief from a patriarchal welfare system. Patriarchy also shapes their attitude to aloneness, and independence may not be seen or valued by the women themselves as a sturdy self-sufficiency. Women without husbands may not relish their personal autonomy but only see the discomforts of their sole responsibilities.

The discussion of women without husbands also contributes to the debate on the complex relationship between families and households. As marriages end or are partially formed families residentially divide. As they divide the differing interests of men, women and children are more clearly visible and the notion of aggregating these becomes more problematic. Their divergent interests can no longer be easily combined. Furthermore these differing interests translate into contrary public policies and the most obvious expression of this is in the courts. Here there is the desire to effect the clean break for adults but to promote the continuation of joint parenting for children. Once families are split, fresh families are hard to accommodate to the nuclear model, as they are undermined by residual interests and former loyalties. Nevertheless the redolence of 'the family' is such that in the formation of second and subsequent families the adult partners have a strong desire to blend into 'proper' families, however incomplete this process may be.

As the ties of family loosen, if not dissolve, other features are revealed. It is at this point that women pay the full cost of caring that they have incurred through marriage. Outside the putative haven of the family they may have to make a living in an economic structure which assumes they have access to male support. In addition, motherhood, as it detaches from wifehood, is reorganised. Women without husbands may specialise in mothering, but the qualities of single parenting are often critically evaluated. They are commonly seen as over-indulgent and, outside 'the family', the care and control of children is seen as problematic. Also in single-parent households the agency of children, so often suppressed in the discussion of socialisation, becomes clearer, and as parenting becomes a more negotiated activity children appear more influential on the relationships of their parents.

The categories of women used as examples within the book, the widowed, the divorced and separated, those with absent husbands and those who cohabit, are diverse. Although they share the common ground of being marital anomalies and encounter similar problems and ambiguities because of this, their social personalities show some variation. Widows are seen as an older group to be pitied where their circumstances are shaped by forces sad but natural. Divorced women and never-married mothers are viewed more critically and this is especially so when children are involved. Lone mothers, especially when they are unmarried, are presently being constructed as the new *bête noires* of the tabloid press. They are seen as leeches on the public purse, using motherhood to draw income support and to jump the housing queue. In the past such women were pilloried for their moral decadence and their sexual delinquency, but contemporary criticism has a stronger monetary flavour.

The ambiguity is marked for women with husbands absent from home, although this group may escape the privations experienced by many women alone. To be wives without the physical presence of a husband creates a marital limbo which many find uncomfortable. They are out of step with both the world of the married and of the single. They have more day-to-day responsibility within a family form that remains patriarchal. For the women who have this less common form of marriage there are other problems. A returning husband has to be accommodated and at least some control over the domestic reins has been relinquished. This women may welcome, or resist and resent.

The book has argued for the elasticity of marriage and the blurring of the legally sharp divide between those women who are married and those who are not. For the cohabiting there is the polemical issue of whether they should be treated as married, of whether the rights and responsibilities of marriage should be extended to this group. In legal terms this hangs about the extent to which customary marriage should be given legal force. The trend has been towards erosion of legal differences between the married and the cohabiting and this is especially so where there are children of the union. But the equation of these states has been universally piecemeal and confused, even in Sweden, one of the few countries to explicitly consider the rights and duties of cohabitants. There is also equivocation in women's groups. Cohabitation can be seen as a way of preserving female autonomy and of constructing more fulfilling but more tenuous links with men. Alternatively cohabitation may lead women to live as married, with all that that implies for day-to-day routines and responsibilities, but without acquiring its benefits. For the divorced there are other sources of ambiguity. Where assumptions of a clean break between husbands and wives is matched with continuing joint custody for mothers and fathers this also ensures that divorce may also be marriage in another form.

These anomalies are part of the long shadow cast by marriage to cover women outside its institutional parameters. It reflects the historic uncertainty about what the identity of women is in relation to men, the home and the workplace. These issues are today no closer to being resolved. The difficulties of these women reflect not problems of being without a husband but the wider issues of the women's place in marriage. As marriage is the main agency for gendering women, its influence is not lost on women who are no longer or not fully married, but merely refracted through their differential circumstances.

As in all aspects of women's lives the experience of their detachment from husbands is mediated by class and ethnicity, factors which are interrelated in Western society. Women from poorer sections of society and from ethnic minorities are disadvantaged, both in and out of marriage, but the issue is broader than this. The whole area is linked to a bourgeois vision of marriage, to which women from other classes and cultural groupings may not subscribe, but against which they are judged..The subject of women without husbands also challenges masculinist approaches to class. As the distance from marriage grows, women's own earnings become more important, but even dissolved relationships with men continue to have a bearing, especially where there is a division of the assets and a question of pension rights. Despite these marital and interpretational differences, the experiences of all women without husbands follow a common thread. All must secure economic and social support, all forge new relationships with children and all accommodate to new household routines.

Although much of the discussion has concentrated on particular groups of women – the widowed, divorced or separated, those who cohabit or are in husband-absent marriages – many of its conclusions can be generalised to all women. Few have no heritage of marriage or domestic connection to men. The gendering of women presumes the normality of conventional family life. The issues of women without husbands are issues of degree rather than clear categorisation, as marriage itself has many dimensions and is central to rules that underpin household organisations, parenting and social and economic support.

At present there are fresh calls to regenerate the family and this has gendered implications. As lone women are increasingly being seen as the delinquents of the welfare state, the concept of bolstering the family and tying their welfare to claims on liable men becomes a means for their control. This may not make any difference to the numbers of women living outside the family, but may worsen their economic and social situation. Any moves to improve their position will attract the criticism that it encourages women to reject 'normal' family life and is tantamount to an attack on the family. One can speculate about the future where women without husbands will continue to be penalised and censured more severely in an effort to force them back inside the family fold or more effectively empowered to be independent. Presently the trend for unmarried mothers appears to be unswervingly 'back to the future' as criticism of them mounts, while for other groups of women without husbands, the continuance of ambiguity in their social and economic lives remains the order of the day.

Bibliography

Abbott, P. and Wallace, C. (1989) 'The family', in *Beyond Thatcherism*, eds P. Brown and R. Sparks (Milton Keynes: Open University Press).

Ahrons, C. and Rodgers, R. (1987) *Divorced Families: A Multidisciplinary Developmental View* (London: Norton & Co).

Alanen, L. (1988) 'Rethinking childhood', *Acta Sociologica*, vol. 31, pt 1, pp. 53–67.

Allan, G. (1979) *The Sociology of Friendship and Kinship* (London: George Allen & Unwin).

Allan, G. (1985) *Family Life* (Oxford: Basil Blackwell).

Anderson, M. (1983) 'How much has the family changed?', *New Society*, 7 October.

Ariès, P. (1981) 'Introduction to part 1', in *Marriage and Remarriage in Populations of the Past*, eds J. Dupâquier, E. Hélin, P. Laslett, M. Livi-Bacci, S. Sogner (London: Academic Press).

Ariès, P. (1985) 'The indissoluble marriage', in *Western Sexuality: Practice and Perception in Past and Present Times*, eds P. Ariès and A. Béjin (Oxford, Blackwell).

Bahr, S. J. (1983) 'Marital dissolution laws: impact of recent changes for women', *Journal of Family Issues*, vol 4, pp. 455–66.

Barrett, M. and McIntosh, M. (1982) *The Anti-Social Family* (London: Verso).

Bayly, C. A. (1981) 'From ritual to ceremony: death ritual and society in Hindu North India since 1600', in J. Whaley, *Mirrors of Mortality: Studies in the Social History of Death* (London: Europa Publications).

Béjin, A. (1985) 'The extra-marital union today', in Ariès and Béjin, *Western Sexuality: Practice and Perception in Past and Present Times* (Oxford: Blackwell).

Bennett, N. G., Bloom, D. E. and Craig, P. H. (1989) 'The divergence of black and white marriage patterns', *American Journal of Sociology*, vol. 95, no. 3 (November) pp. 692–722.

Berger, P. and Berger, B. (1983) *The War Over the Family* (London: Hutchinson).

Berger, P. L. and Kellner, H. (1980) 'Marriage and construction of reality', in M. Anderson (ed.), *The Sociology of the Family* (Harmondsworth: Penguin) pp. 1–23.

Bernard, J. (1972) *The Future of Marriage* (New York: Souvenir Press).

Binney, V., Harkell, G. and Nixon, J. (1985) 'Refuges and housing for battered women', in *Private Violence and Public Policy*, ed. J. Pahl (London: Routledge & Kegan Paul).

Blaxter, M. (1989) *Health and Life Style* (London: Tavistock).

Boulton, M. G. (1983) *On Being a Mother* (London: Tavistock).

Bowling, A. and Cartwright, A. (1982) *Life After Death* (London: Tavistock).

Bradshaw, J. (1989) *Lone Parents: Policy in the Doldrums* (London: Family Policy Centre).

Brittan, A. and Maynard, M. (1984) *Sexism, Racism and Oppression* (Oxford: Basil Blackwell).

Brophy, B. (1989) 'Custody law, child care and inequality in Britain', in *Child Custody and the Politics of Gender*, eds C. Smart and S. Sevenhuijsen (London: Routledge).

174

Brown, G. and Harris, T. (1978) *The Social Origins of Depression: A Study of Psychiatric Disorder in Women* (London: Tavistock).

Bulmer, M. (1986) *Neighbours: The Work of Philip Abrams* (Cambridge: Cambridge University Press).

Burgoyne, J. (1984) *Breaking Even: Divorce, You and Your Children* (Harmondsworth: Penguin).

Burgoyne, J. (1986) 'Recent changes in gender-based patterns of employment, partnership and family formation: some theoretical and methodological implications of this challenge to conventional conceptualisations of the family life cycle', paper given at the British Sociological Conference, Loughborough.

Burgoyne, J. and Clark, D. (1984) *Making a Go of It* (London: Routledge & Kegan Paul).

Burgoyne, J., Ormrod, R. and Richards, M. (1987) *Divorce Matters* (Harmondsworth: Penguin).

Busfield, J. (1983) 'Gender, mental illness and psychiatry', in *Sexual Divisions: Patterns and Processes*, eds M. Evans and C. Ungerson (London: Tavistock).

Callan, H. and Ardener, S. (eds) (1984) *The Incorporated Wife* (London: Croom Helm).

Cashmore, E. E. (1985) *Having To: The World of One-Parent Families* (London: Counterpoint, Unwin).

Chandler, J. (1987) 'Sailors' wives and husband absence', unpublished thesis, Plymouth Polytechnic.

Chandler, J. (1989) 'The marriage and housing careers of naval wives', *Sociological Review*, vol. 37, pp. 253–76.

Charles, N. and Kerr, M. (1988) *Women, Food and Families* (Manchester: Manchester University Press).

Cherlin, A. (1978) 'Remarriage as an incomplete institution', *American Journal of Sociology*, vol. 84, pp. 634–50.

Chester, R. (1972) 'Divorce and legal aid: a false hypothesis', *Sociology*, vol. 6, pp. 205–16.

Chester, R. (1985) 'The rise of the neo-conventional family', *New Society*, 9 May.

Clark, D., McCann, K., Morrice, K. and Taylor, R. (1985) 'Work and marriage in the off-shore oil industry', *International Journal of Social Economics*, vol. 12, pt. 2, pp. 36–47.

Clark, E. (1989) *Young Single Mothers Today: A Qualitative Study of Housing and Support Needs* (London: National Council for One Parent Families).

Cohen, G. (ed.) (1987) *Social Change and the Life Course* (London: Tavistock).

Collins, R. (1990) 'Unmarried parenthood and the law: upholding the nuclear family', a paper given at the BSA Conference, Guildford.

Cornwell, J. (1984) *Hard-Earned Lives: Accounts of Health and Illness from East London* (London: Tavistock).

Cotton, S., Anthill, J. and Cunningham, J. (1983) 'Living together: before, instead of and after marriage', in *The Family in the Modern World: Australian Perspectives*, eds A. Burns, G. Bottomley and P. Jools (Sydney: Allen & Unwin).

Coveney, L., Jackson, M., Jeffreys, S., Kay, L. and Mahony, P. (1984) *The Sexuality Papers*, Explorations in Feminism (London: Hutchinson).

Davidoff, L and Hall, C. (1987) *Family Fortunes* (London: Hutchinson).

Davis, G., MacLeod, A. and Murch, M. (1982) 'Divorce and the resolution of conflict', *Law Society Gazette*, 13 January, pp. 40–1.

Deem, R. (1987) 'My husband says I'm too old for dancing', in *Women and the Life Cycle: Transitions and Turning Points*, eds P. Allatt, T. Keil, B. Bytheway and A. Bryman (Basingstoke: Macmillan).

Delphy, C. (1984) *Close to Home* (London: Hutchinson).

Dex, S. and Shaw, L. B. (1988) 'Women's working lives: a comparison of women in the United States and Great Britain', in *Women and Paid Work*, ed. A. Hunt (Basingstoke: Macmillan).

Donzelot, J. (1980) *The Policing of Families* (London: Hutchinson).

Douglas, M. (1970) *Purity and Danger* (Harmondsworth: Penguin).

Douglas, M. (1972) 'Deciphering a meal', *Daedalus*, vol. 101, pp. 61–81.

Durkheim, E. (1952) *Suicide* (London: Routledge & Kegan Paul).

Edgell, S. (1980) *Middle Class Couples: A Study of Segregation, Domination and Inequality in Marriage* (London: George Allen & Unwin).

Edwards, S. (1987) ' "Provoking her own demise": from common assault to homicide', in *Women, Violence and Social Control*, eds J. Hanmer and M. Maynard (Basingstoke: Macmillan).

Eekelaar, J. and Maclean, M. (1986) *Maintenance After Divorce* (Oxford: Clarendon Press).

Elder, G. H. (1978) 'Family history and the life course', in *Transitions: The Family and the Life Course in Historical Perspective*, ed. T. K. Hareven (New York: Academic Press) pp. 17–64.

Evans-Pritchard, E. E. (1990) *Kinship and Marriage Among the Nuer* (Oxford: Oxford University Press).

Evason, E. (1980) *Just Me and the Kids: A Study of Single Parent Families in Northern Ireland* (Equal Opportunities Commission for Northern Ireland).

Farley, R. and Allen, W. (1987) *The Color Line and the Quality of Life in America* (New York: Russell Sage).

Fennell, G., Phillipson, C and Evers, H. (1988) *The Sociology of Old Age* (Milton Keynes: Open University Press).

Finch, J. (1983) *Married to the Job* (London: Allen & Unwin).

Finch, J. (1989) *Family Obligations and Social Change* (Cambridge: Polity Press).

Finch, J. and Mason, J. (1989) 'Divorce, remarriage and family obligations', a paper given to the British Sociological Association, Plymouth Polytechnic.

Fineman, M. L. (1989) 'The politics of custody and gender: child advocacy and the transformation of custody decision-making and the USA', in *Child Custody and the Politics of Gender*, eds C. Smart and S. Sevenhuijsen (London: Routledge).

Fletcher, R. (1988a) *The Shaking of the Foundations: Family and Society* (London: Routledge & Kegan Paul).

Fletcher, R. (1988b) *The Abolitionists: The Family and Marriage Under Attack* (London: Routledge).

Franks, H. (1988) *Remarriage: What Makes It And What Breaks It* (London: Bodley Head).

Freeman, M. D. and Lyon, C. M. (1983) *Cohabitation Without Marriage* (Aldershot: Gower).

Furstenberg, F. F. and Spanier, G. (1984) *Recycling the Family* (London: Sage).

Gerstel, N. (1988) 'Divorce and kin ties: the importance of gender', *Journal of Marriage and the Family*, vol. 50 (February).

Gillis, J. R. (1985) *For Better, For Worse: British Marriages 1600 to the Present* (Oxford: Oxford University Press).

Gittins, D. (1985) *The Family in Question* (Basingstoke: Macmillan).

Glick, P. C. (1979) 'Children of divorced parents in demographic perspective', *Journal of Social Issues*, vol. 35, pt. 4, pp. 170–82.

Glyptis, S. and McInnes, H. (1987) *Leisure and the Home* (London: Sports Council).

Gorer, G. (1965) *Death, Grief and Mourning* (London: Cresset).

Graham, H. (1987) 'Being poor: perceptions and coping strategies of lone mothers', in *Give and Take in Families: Studies in Resource Distribution* eds J. Brannen and G. Wilson (London: Allen & Unwin).

Greer, G. (1985) *Sex and Destiny: The Politics of Human Fertility* (London: Picador).

Gross, H. E. (1987) 'Couples who live apart; time/place disjunctions and their consequences', in *Women and Symbolic Interactionism*, eds M. J. Deegan and M. Hill (London: Allen & Unwin).

Groves, D. (1987) 'Occupational pension provision and women's poverty in old age', in *Women and Poverty in Britain*, eds C. Glendenning and J. Millar (Brighton: Wheatsheaf).

Gutman, H. G. (1976) *The Black Family in Slavery and Freedom 1750–1925* (Oxford: Basil Blackwell).

Halem, L. C. (1982) *Separated and Divorced Women* (Connecticut: Greenwood Press).

Hanawalt, B. A. (1986) *The Ties That Bind: Peasant Families in Medieval England* (Oxford: Oxford University Press).

Hardey, M. (1989) 'Lone parents and the home', in *Home and the Family: Creating the Domestic Sphere*, eds G. Allan and G. Crow (London: Macmillan).

Hareven, T. K. (1982) *Family Time and Industrial Time: The Relationship Between the Family and Work in a New England Industrial Community* (Cambridge: Cambridge University Press).

Harris, C. C. (1983) *The Family and Industrial Society* (London: Allen & Unwin).

Haskey, J. (1987) 'Trends in marriage and divorce in England and Wales: 1837–1987', *Population Trends*, no. 48 (Summer).

Haskey, J. (1989) 'One parent families and their children in Great Britain: numbers and characteristics', *Populations Trends*, no. 55 (Spring).

Haskey, J. and Coleman, D. (1986) 'Cohabitation before marriage: a comparison of information from marriage registration and the General Household Survey', *Populations Trends*, no. 43 (Spring).

Hite, S. (1987) *Women and Love: A Cultural Revolution in Progress* (Harmondsworth: Penguin).

Hoem, B. and Hoem, J. (1988) 'The Swedish family: aspects of contemporary developments', *Journal of Family Issues*, vol. 9, no. 3.

Hofferth, S. L. (1985) 'Updating children's life course', *Journal of Marriage and the Family*, vol. 47, pp. 93–115.

Holme, A. (1985) *Housing and Young Families in East London* (London: Routledge & Kegan Paul).

Hunt, P. (1989) 'Gender and the construction of home life', in *Home and Family: Creating the Domestic Sphere*, eds G. Allan and G. Crow (London: Macmillan).

Ihinger-Tallman, M. and Pasley K. (1987) *Remarriage*, Family Studies Text Series 7 (Beverley Hills: Sage).

Imray, L. and Middleton, A. (1983) 'Public and private: marking the boundaries', in *the Public and the Private*, ed. E. Garmarnikov (London: Heinemann).

Isay, R. A. (1968) 'The submariners' wives syndrome', *Psychiatric Quarterly*, vol. 42, pp. 647–52.

Jenks, C. (ed.) (1982) *The Sociology of Childhood: Essential Readings* (London: Batsford Academic and Educational)

John, A. V. (1980) *By the Sweat of Their Brow: Women Workers and the Victorian Coal Mines* (Trowbridge: Redwood Burn).

Joshi, H. (1987) 'The cost of caring', in *Women and Poverty in Britain*, eds C. Glendinning and J. Millar (Brighton: Wheatsheaf).

Kaslow, F. W. and Schartz, L. L. (1987) *The Dynamics of Divorce: A Life Cycle*

Perspective (New York: Brunner-Mazel).

Kiernan, K. and Wicks, M. (1990) *Family Change and Future Policy* (York: Family Policy Studies Centre/Joseph Rowntree Memorial Trust).

Komarovsky, M. (1962) *Blue Collar Marriage* (New York: Random House).

Laing, R. D. and Esterson, A. (1970) *Sanity, Madness and the Family* (Harmondsworth: Penguin).

Land, H. (1975) 'The myth of the male breadwinner', *New Society*, vol. 34, no. 679 (October).

Land, H. (1980) 'The family wage', *Feminist Review*, vol. 6, pp. 55–78.

Lasch, C. (1977) *Haven in a Heartless World* (New York: Basic Books).

Lasch, C. (1979) *The Culture of Narcissism: American Life in an Age of Diminishing Expectations* (New York: Basic Books).

Laslett, P. (1972) 'The history of the family', in *Household and Family in Past Times*, ed. P. Laslett and R. Wall (Cambridge: Cambridge University Press).

Laslett, P. (1977) *Family Life and Illicit Love in Earlier Generations* (Cambridge: Cambridge University Press).

Law Commission (1986) *Review of Child Law: Custody* (London: HMSO).

Lawson, A. (1989) *Adultery: An Analysis of Love and Betrayal* (Oxford: Blackwell).

Lebsock, S. (1983) 'Free black women and the question of matriarchy', in *Sex and Class in History*, eds J. L. Newton, M. P. Ryan and J. R. Walkowitz (London: Routledge & Kegan Paul).

Lees, S. (1986) *Losing Out: Sexuality and Adolescent Girls* (London: Hutchinson).

Lewis, J. and Meredith, B. (1988) *Daughters Who Care* (London: Routledge).

Lewis, J. and Piachaud, D. (1987) 'Women and poverty in the twentieth century', in *Women and Poverty in Britain*, eds C. Glendenning and J. Millar (Brighton: Wheatsheaf).

Logan, F. (1987) *Homelessness and Relationship Breakdown: A Study of the Law and Social Policy in Relation to Women and Housing* (London: National Council for One Parent Families).

Lund, M. (1984) 'Research on divorce and children', *Family Law*, vol. 14, pp. 198–201.

Lynes, T. (1986) 'Welfare watch', *New Society*, vol. 48 (17 Oct.).

McCoy, K. F. and Nelson, M. A. (1983) *Social Service Departments and Matrimonial Causes (NI) Order* (Belfast: Social Work Advisory Group).

Macfarlane, A. (1978) *The Origins of English Individualism* (Oxford: Basil Blackwell).

Macfarlane, A. (1986) *Marriage and Love in England 1300–1840* (Oxford: Basil Blackwell).

McKee, L. (1982) 'Fathers' participation in infant care', in *Father Figure*, eds L. McKee and M. O'Brien (London: Tavistock).

McKee, L. and Bell, C. (1986) 'His unemployment: her problem: the domestic and marital consequences of male unemployment', in *The Experience of Unemployment*, eds S. Allen, A. Waton, K. Purcell and S. Wood (Basingstoke).

Macklin, E. D. (1983) 'Non-marital cohabitation: an overview', in *Contemporary Families and Alternative Lifestyles: A Handbook of Research and Theory*, eds E. D. Macklin and R. H. Rubin (Beverley Hills: Sage).

McLanahan, S., Wedeymer, N. and Adelberg, T. (1981) 'Network structure, social support and psychological well-being in single-parent families', *Journal of Marriage and the Family*, vol. 43, pp. 601–12.

Maclean, M. (1987) 'Households after divorce: the availability of resources and their impact on children' in *Give and Take in Families: Studies in Resource Distribution* eds J. Brannen and G. Wilson (London: Allen & Unwin).

Macmillan, M. (1984) 'Camp followers: a note on the wives of the armed forces', in

The Incorporated Wife, eds H. Callan and S. Ardener (London: Croom Helm).
Mansfield, P. and Collard, J. (1988) *The Beginning of the Rest of Your Life?* (Basingstoke: Macmillan).
Martin, B. (1984) 'Mother wouldn't like it: housework as magic', *Theory, Culture and Society*, vol. 2, pt. 2, pp. 19–36.
Martin, J. and Roberts, C. (1984) *Women and Employment: A Lifetime Perspective* (DE/OPCS).
Martinez-Alier, V. (1974) *Marriage, Class and Colour in Nineteenth Century Cuba: A Study of Racial Attitudes and Sexual Values in Slave Society* (Cambridge: Cambridge University Press).
Mason, J. (1987) ' "A bed of roses?" Women, marriage and inequality in later life', in *Women and the Life Cycle: Transitions and Turning Points*, eds P. Allatt, T. Keil, B. Bytheway and A. Bryman (London: Macmillan).
Menefee, S. P. (1981) *Wives for Sale*. (Oxford: Basil Blackwell).
Miles, A. (1988) *Women and Mental Illness: The Social Context of Female Madness* (Brighton: Wheatsheaf).
Millar, J. (1987) 'Lone mothers', in *Women and Poverty in Britain*, eds C. Glendinning and J. Millar (Brighton: Wheatsheaf).
Millar, J. and Glendinning, C. (1987) 'Invisible women, invisible poverty', in *Women and Poverty in Britain*, eds C. Glendinning and J. Millar (Brighton: Wheatsheaf).
Mitchell, A. (1985) *Children in the Middle – Living Through Divorce* (London: Tavistock).
Moore, H. L. (1988) *Feminism and Anthropology* (Cambridge: Polity Press).
Morgan, D. H. J. (1985) *The Family, Politics and Social Theory* (London: Routledge & Kegan Paul).
Morrice, J. K. W. (1981) 'Psycho-social problems in the oil industry', *Update*, vol. 22, pp. 27–34.
Morrice, J. K. W., Taylor, R. C., Clark, D and McCann, K. (1985) 'Oil wives and intermittent husbands', *British Journal of Psychiatry*, vol. 147, pp. 479–83.
Mount, F. (1982) *The Subversive Family* (London: Counterpoint, Unwin).
Murcott, A. (1983) ' "It's a pleasure to cook for him." Food, mealtimes and gender in some South Wales households', in *The Public and the Private* eds E. Garmarnikov *et al*. (London: Heinemann).
Murphy, M. J. (1983) *The Life Course of Individuals in the Family: Describing Static and Dynamic Aspects of the Contemporary Family*, OPCS Occasional Paper 31.
Murray, C. (1981) *Families Divided: The Impact of Migrant Labour in Lesotho* (Cambridge: Cambridge University Press).
National Council for One Parent Families (1984) *Time-off for Child-Care* (London).
National Council for One Parent Families in Britain (1987) *Black One-Parent Families in Britain* (London).
National Council for One Parent Families (1990) *Barriers to Work: A Study of Lone Parents' Training and Employment* (London).
Needham, R. (1971) 'Introduction' in *Rethinking Kinship and Marriage*, ed. R. Needham, Association of Social Anthropologists, Monograph II (London: Tavistock).
Nicholson, P. J. (1980) *Goodbye Sailor: The Importance of Friendship in Family Mobility and Separation* (Inverness: Northpress Ltd).
Oakley, A. (1982) *Subject Women* (London: Martin Robinson).
Oakley, A. (1984) *Taking it Like a Woman* (London: Flamingo, Fontana Press).
OPCS (1989) *General Household Survey* (London: HMSO).
OPCS (1989) *Population Trends*, vol. 57 (London: HMSO).
Orbach, S and Eichenbaum, L. (1988) *Bittersweet* (London: Arrow Books).

Pahl, J. (1980) 'Patterns of money management within marriage', *Journal of Social Policy*, vol. 9, pp. 313–35.

Pahl, J. (1985) 'Violent husbands and abused wives: a longitudinal study', in *Private Violence and Public Policy: The Needs of Battered Women and the Response of the Public Services*, ed. J. Pahl, (London: Routledge & Kegan Paul) pp. 23–94.

Pahl, R. E. (1984) *Divisions of Labour* (Oxford: Blackwell).

Parker, G. (1985) *With Due Care and Attention* (London: Family Policy Studies Centre).

Parkes, C. M. (1975) *Bereavement: Studies in Grief in Adult Life* (Harmondsworth: Pelican).

Parkinson, L. (1986) *Conciliation in Separation and Divorce* (Beckenham: Croom Helm).

Parkinson, L. (1987) *Separation, Divorce and Families* (Basingstoke: Macmillan).

Popay, J., Rimmer, L. and Rossiter, C. (1983) *One Parent Families: Parents, Children and Public Policy* (London: Study Commission on the Family, Occasional Paper No. 12).

Popenhoe, D. (1987) 'Beyond the nuclear family: a statistical portrait of the changing family in Sweden', *Journal of Marriage and the Family*, vol. 49, pp. 173–83.

Porter, M. (1983) 'Women and old boats: sexual division of labour in a Newfoundland outport', in *The Public and the Private*, ed. E. Gamarnikov (London: Heinemann).

Prior, L. (1989) *The Social Organisation of Death: Medical Discourse and Social Practice in Belfast* (Basingstoke: Macmillan).

Qvortrop, J. (1985) 'Placing children in the division of labour', in *Family and Economy*, eds P. Close and R. Collins (London: Macmillan).

Rapoport, R. N. and Rapoport, R. (1982) 'British families in transition', in *Families in Britain*, eds R. N. Rapoport, M. P. Rapoport, M. P. Fogarty and R. Rapoport (London: Routledge & Kegan Paul).

Robins, P. K. (1986) 'Child support, welfare dependency and poverty', *American Economic Review*, vol. 76 (September).

Ross, E. (1983) 'Survival networks: women's neighbourhood sharing in London before World War I', *History Workshop*, issue 15 (Spring).

Rubin, L. B. (1976) *Worlds of Pain* (New York: Basic Books).

Rubin, L. B. (1983) *Just Friends: The Role of Friendship in Our Lives* (New York: Harper & Row).

Sarantakos, S. (1984) *Living Together in Australia* (Melbourne: Longman Cheshire).

Schofield, R. and Wrigley, E. A. (1981) 'Remarriage intervals and the effect of marriage order on fertility', in *Marriage and Remarriage in Populations of the Past*, eds J. Dupâquier, E. Hélin, P. Laslett, M. Livi-Bacci and S. Sogner (London: Academic Press).

Schuetz, A. (1945) 'The homecomer', *American Journal of Sociology*, vol. 50.

Seltzer, J. A. (1989) 'Relationships between fathers and children who live apart', National Survey of Families and Households, Working Paper No. 4, Center for Demography and Ecology, University of Wisconsin, cited in *Family Change and Future Policy*, eds K. Kiernan and M. Wicks (York: Family Policy Studies Centre/Joseph Rowntree Memorial Trust).

Shahar, S. (1983) *The Fourth Estate: A History of Women in the Middle Ages* (London: Methuen).

Shuchter, S. R. (1986) *Dimensions of Grief: Adjusting to the Death of the Spouse* (London: Jossey-Bass).

Smart, C. (1984) *The Ties That Bind* (London: Routlege & Kegan Paul).
Smart, C. (1987) 'Securing the family', in *The State or the Market: Politics and Welfare in Contemporary Britain* ed. M. Looney (London: Sage).
Smart, C. (1989) 'Power and the politics of child custody', *Child Custody and the Politics of Gender*, eds C. Smart and S. Sevenhuijsen (London: Routledge).
Smart, C and Sevenhuijsen, S. (1989) *Child Custody and the Politics of Gender* (London: Routledge).
Smith, R. T. (1988) *Kinship and Class in the West Indies* (Cambridge: Cambridge University Press).
Smith, S. (1986) 'The wife's sentence', *New Society*, 21 November.
Social Trends (1989) Central Statistical Office (London: HMSO).
Social Trends (1990) Central Statistical Office (London: HMSO).
Sogner, S. and Dupâquier, J. (1981) 'Introduction' to *Marriage and Remarriage in Populations of the Past*, eds J. Dupâquier, E. Hélin, P. Laslett, M. Livi-Bacci and S. Sogner (London: Academic Press).
Solheim, J. (1984) 'Off-shore commuting and family adaptation in the local community', a paper read at the International Conference on Oil and the Environment, Bergen.
Spensky, M. (1989) 'From the workhouse to the home for unmarried mothers: a feminist perspective', a paper delivered at the British Sociological Association Conference, Plymouth Polytechnic.
Stamp, P. (1985) 'Research note: balance of financial power in marriage: an exploratory study of bread-winning wives', *Sociological Review*, vol. 33, no. 3 (August).
Stone, L. (1977) *The Family, Sex and Marriage in England 1500–1800* (London: Weidenfeld & Nicholson).
Sullivan, O. (1986) 'Housing movements of the divorced and separated', *Housing Studies*, vol. 1, no. 1 (January).
Taylor, R., Morrice, K., Clark, D and McCann, K. (1985) 'The psycho-social consequences of intermittent husband absence: an epidemiological study', *Social Science and Medicine*, vol. 20, no. 9, pp. 877–85.
Thane, P. (1978) 'Women and the Poor Law in Victorian and Edwardian England', *History Workshop*, no. 6 (Autumn).
Thèry, I. (1989) ' "The interest of the child" and the regulation of the post-divorce family', in *Child Custody and the Politics of Gender* eds C. Smart and S. Sevenhuijsen (London: Routledge).
Thompson, P., Wailey, T. and Lummis, T. (1983) *Living the Fishing* (London: Routledge & Kegan Paul).
Thorogood, N. (1987) 'Race and gender: the politics of housework', in *Give and Take in Families: Studes in Resource Distribution*, eds J. Brannen and G. Wilson (London: Allen & Unwin).
Tietjen, A. (1985) 'The social networks and social support of married and single mothers in Sweden', *Journal of Marriage and the Family*, vol. 47, pp. 489–96.
Tilly, L. and Scott, J. (1978) *Women, Work and the Family* (London: Holt, Rinehart & Winston).
Tinker, I. (1981) 'New technologies for food-related activities: an equity strategy, in *Women and Technological Change in Developing Countries* (Boulder, Colorado: Westview Press).
Troph, W. D. (1984) 'An exploratory examination of the effects of remarriage on child support and personal contact', *Journal of Divorce*, vol. 7, pp. 57–73.
Trost, J. E. (1985) 'Marital and non-marital cohabitation', in *The Nordic Family: Perspectives on Family Research*, Essays in Social and Demographic History, eds J. Rogers and H. Norman (Uppsala University).

Trustram, M. (1984) *Women of the Regiment: Marriage and the Victorian Army* (Cambridge: Cambridge University Press).

Tunstall, J. (1962) *The Fishermen* (London: MacGibbon & Kee).

Ungerson, C. (1987) *Policy is Personal: Sex, Gender and Informal Care* (London: Tavistock).

Walby, S. (1986) *Patriarchy at Work* (Cambridge: Polity Press).

Walby, S. (1990) *Theorising Patriarchy* (Oxford: Basil Blackwell).

Walker, A. (1987) ' "The poor relation": poverty among old women', in *Women and Poverty in Britain*, eds C. Glendinning and J. Millar (Brighton: Wheatsheaf).

Walker, C. and Walker, A. (1986) *The Growing Divide: A Social Audit* (London: CPAG).

Wallace, C. (1987) 'From generation to generation: the effects of employment and unemployment upon the domestic life cycle of young adults', in *Education, Unemployment and Labour Markets*, eds P. Brown and N. A. Ashton (Brighton: Falmer Press).

Wallerstein, J. S. and Kelly, J. B. (1980) *Surviving the Break-Up* (London: Grant McIntyre).

Waters, M. (1989) 'Patriarchy and viriarchy: an exploration and reconstruction of concepts of masculine domination', *Sociology*, vol. 23, no. 2 (May).

Weiss, R. S. (1979) *Going it Alone: The Family Life and Social Situation of the Single Parent* (New York: Basic Books).

Weitzman, L. J. (1985) *The Divorce Revolution: The Unexpected Social and Economic Consequences for Women and Children in America* (New York: Free Press).

Whitehead, A. (1976) 'Sexual antagonism in Herefordshire', in *Dependence and Exploitation in Work and Marriage* eds D. Barker and S. Allen (London: Longman).

Willmott, P. (1986) *Social Networks, Informal Care and Public Policy* (London: Policy Studies Institute).

Wilson, G. (1987) 'Money: patterns of responsibility and irresponsibility in marriage', in *Give and Take in Families: Studies in Resource Distribution* eds J. Brannen and G. Wilson (London: Allen & Unwin).

Wolfram, S. (1987) *In-laws and Out-laws: Kinship and Marriage in England* (London: Croom Helm).

Wylie, B. J. (1986) *Beginnings: A Book for Widows* (London: Unwin).

Young, M and Willmott, P. (1962) *Family and Kinship in East London* (Harmondsworth: Penguin).

Zaretsky, E. (1982) 'The place of the family in the origins of the welfare state', in *Rethinking the Family*, eds B. Thorne and M. Yalom (London: Longman).

Index